HER
GAME
TOO

Matthew Riley

HER GAME TOO

A MANIFESTO
FOR CHANGE

First published by Pitch Publishing, 2022

Pitch Publishing
9 Donnington Park,
85 Birdham Road,
Chichester,
West Sussex,
PO20 7AJ
www.pitchpublishing.co.uk
info@pitchpublishing.co.uk

ISBN 978 1 80150 208 5

Typesetting and origination by Pitch Publishing
Printed and bound in Great Britain by TJ Books Limited

Contents

For Karen.

Nothing else matters

Foreword by Tracey Crouch MP

PROUDLY REPRESENTING Chatham and Aylesford as their MP, and as author of November 2021's Fan-Led Review of Football Governance, I am delighted to endorse *Her Game Too: A Manifesto for Change.* As the book describes, the women's game is at a crossroads after experiencing huge growth, and needs to face some legacy issues that must be addressed urgently. As we wait for a separate review into women's football to fully consider the issues at play, this book will help keep the momentum going for the huge strides that have been made in the women's game since the dark days of 1921 when women's football was banned.

Campaigning groups like Her Game Too and Women in Football have helped drive the development of the women's game, while addressing some of the misogynistic and blinkered attitudes to women playing, commentating on, following, officiating, coaching and administering the beautiful game. Thankfully, groups like these and the majority of fans have pushed these attitudes into the margins and have helped inspire a new generation of girls and women to take up footballing careers across a widening range of roles.

I grew up in the eighties when it wasn't the done thing for girls to play football. I was constantly being stopped from playing in the playground at primary school and then I went to an all-girls' school where it was an option for PE. I doubt there were any local girls' teams but because there was no coverage of women's football, I didn't even know to look for them. It wasn't until I got to university that I played my first game of competitive football. Switching from playing to coaching at the age of 30 enabled me to give something back to the game, staying with the same girls' team in Chatham from under-10s to ladies. I could never quite help myself, though, and regularly reminded them how lucky they were to live in a time and a country where girls could play football.

As I shared with the Digital Culture Media and Sport Committee on 7 December 2021, I played football with girls in Saudi Arabia and engaged with their sports minister. It was heartening to see a picture in *The Times* of a Saudi female national player showing her skills in their national stadium. Football has a massive part to play in promoting human rights globally. I was humbled to captain the parliamentary team against the Afghan Women's Development team in March 2022. These were girls who needed to be rescued from the Taliban simply because they played sport. Football is an international language and these girls, most of them just in their teens, were fluent.

When collecting evidence for my report, it was clear that many fans, both male and female, wanted the women's game to avoid the mistakes being made in the men's. That is why we need a manifesto for change. A clear pathway to watching, supporting and running football that is sustainable, equitable, empowering and collaborative.

Her Game Too: A Manifesto for Change explores a values-based approach that promotes fairness and integrity not only between the men's and women's game, but within the women's game itself. There are, as I noted in my review, signs of overheating at some top WSL clubs in a league celebrating its first decade this year and which has been fully professional since the 2018/19 season. I heard a lot of evidence of concern that the gap between the top of the game and the FA National Women's League was growing, but there is also great determination to keep the women's game equitable. The book calls for an open and transparent approach to the women's game. This is also an area they can learn from reviewing the mistakes often made in the men's game, where certain practices have helped circumvent protective measures such as Financial Fair Play and profitability and sustainability rules. The negative consequences of the Elite Player Performance Plan being put together for lower league men's clubs are another learning point that the women's game can consider.

Other appalling omissions can be addressed immediately. When Sam Kerr barged over a pitch invader in December 2021 during Chelsea Women's Champions League tie against Juventus, she was given a yellow card and he was not arrested. The reason? Under section four of the 1991 Football (Offences) Act, it is an arrestable offence to go onto the playing area. The law states: 'It is an offence for a person at a designated football match to go onto the playing area, or any area adjacent to the playing area to which spectators are not generally admitted, without lawful authority or lawful excuse (which shall be for him to prove).' A person guilty of this offence is liable to a fine of up to £1,000.

However, this legislation only applies to 'designated matches' and Women's Champions League and Women's Super League games are not considered to be in that category. According to the Football (Offences) (Designation of Football Matches) Order 2004, a designated match is 'a game in which one or both of the teams represents a club which is a member of the English Football League, the Premier League, the Football Conference or the League of Wales, or represents a country or territory'. This list excludes women's games and is something that, by the time this book is released, will surely be a loophole that is consigned to history.

As the men's game continues to feel the repercussions of Project Big Picture and the European Super League, the women's game has a fantastic opportunity to foster the unique selling point of a community-focussed and inclusive ethos for all levels of the game. One of the chapters in this book highlights the Her Game Too weekend at Exeter City last season, where the whole club celebrated the women's game during 48 hours of shared values. The Exeter City Women's game attracted more fans than Chelsea Women would see that week for a Champions League game, showing the huge benefits of a one-club approach. City also beat local rivals Plymouth Argyle on penalties, so sales of Thatchers cider performed very healthily after the game, I hear!

As the book looks back on a decade since the appalling comments made by Richard Keys and Andy Gray, we must inspire and promote positively rather than (understandably) berate and criticise the behaviour of the game's often male, pale and stale custodians that have consistently failed to show respect or support for women trying to make their way in the game. There are historical role models like Lily Parr, contemporary ones like Jacqui Oatley, Ellen White and Susan Whelan, and a growing movement to make women's football a powerful force for good in sport and a beacon for fairness in wider society. That is why I believe the separate review of women's football will give focus and foster growth.

Her Game Too: A Manifesto for Change will raise awareness and funds for the Exeter City Women's team. I am delighted to help support it.

The Euros: See It and Be It

Before we start, let's take a moment to pause, draw breath and shout out our proudest, loudest Lioness roar. Wow! Just. Absolutely. Wow! The last time England lifted a trophy women were banned from even playing but this group of affable, relatable and highly skilled players have blazed trails that will be followed for generations to come. Matt goes into more detail about this seminal moment for women's football, but I just wanted to add my thanks to the volunteers, coaches, fans, support staff and players that have battled long odds for generations and laid the foundations for a golden future for the game. This is your time and you have put a spring in the step of a nation. Here to play and here to stay.

Writing in November 2021, University of Madrid Professor Celia Valiente produced a study of Spanish football that also raised important global issues. Called, 'Sport Mega-Events and the Search for Gender Equality' it sees tournaments like the Euros as strong drivers and resources for equality, but for meaningful change, they also need to send out a strong message to policy makers that women create added sporting, economic and societal value. This is why I have called for a separate fan-led review of the women's game to help maintain the momentum currently enjoyed. The 'see it and be it' opportunities, particularly with England's media-friendly, personable squad will create a new generation of aspirational young girls and women who use the tournament as launch pads for their own dreams. Valiente also draws attention to how 'mega-events' generate and distribute a huge mainstream media profile that helps the sport break out of a vicious circle of, 'low coverage of women's sport and small audiences of women's athletic competitions.' Or, as Suzanne Wrack describes it in her excellent book, *A Woman's Game: The Rise, Fall, and Rise Again of Women's Football*:

> 'International tournaments have aided this work, acting as catalysts for growth, driving participation numbers and investment, domestically. Success and progress breed success and progress; if clubs and national football associations taste even the possibility of silverware or of a commercially lucrative opportunity they will bite. And with each tournament cycle, the game is pushed a step forward.'

Tournaments like the Euros also help highlight how gender equality in society has strong links to success for national women's teams. In July, author Michael Cox reviewed the rewards for countries like the Nordic nations, all five of which (if we don't consider the Faroe Islands with a FIFA rank of 99 and unranked Greenland) qualified for the finals. Cox offers two key reasons for the north/south divide. The obvious one is their generally stronger economies. But there is more. Cox highlights the incredible overachievement of the Nordic countries by population, having only 28 million people which, he points out, is 'roughly one-third of the population of Germany's 83 million' that sees them punching hugely above their population weight. But rather than being mice that roar, the Nordic countries generally showed, according to 2020's World Economic Forum report, (with the surprising exception of Denmark) high levels of gender equality in areas such as the economy, education, health and politics.

More widely, of the 16 qualifiers, only Italy is outside the Global Gender Gap report top 40 and is struggling to stay successful in the ever-increasing rise of professionalism in surrounding countries. The message this data gives is hugely empowering and describes a virtuous circle of female inclusion in society helping to sustain and drive better outcomes for everyone and, as a flag bearer of the process, their women's national team.

Reviewing the FIFA ranking and progress of each country, the scarcity of surprising failures or success suggests the system has matured into a relatively accurate predictor of how teams will fare. The eight teams who failed to make it past the group stages included the three lowest-ranked teams, Northern Ireland, Portugal and Finland, and the average FIFA rank of those who failed to qualify was 19. Austria and Belgium managed to survive, despite having lower FIFA rankings than four other countries that failed at the first hurdle, Iceland, Denmark, Italy and Norway, before being knocked out in the quarter-finals as the only two countries left outside the top ten. The four who failed at the quarter-final stage averaged 13, while the four who progressed averaged four FIFA places.

Wherever we look there is evidence supporting the organic, dynamic and exponential rise of women's football. Records for viewing figures, participation and media profile fall with increasing speed, backed by strident support from campaigns like Hope United, which sends out powerful messages of equality, diversity and inclusion driven by high-profile role models within the game. The range of support networks for the women's game is growing exponentially. One exceptional example is Equal Playing Field, a campaign lobbying for a grassroots and branch approach to furthering access, opportunity, acceptance and value for female players. These key aims all feed into the wonderful work of Her Game Too and the family of sister organisations fuelling a journey from bizarre exclusion to everyday equality. There are some concerning signs of overheating and there is a clear need to support the profile of talented BAME (Black, Asian and minority ethnic) players to carry on the stunning progress made by Hope Powell that is explored later in the book, but it is better trying to put out fires than desperately looking to fan a spark.

The last word, for now, needs to come from Sarina Wiegman:

'Play for the little girl that wanted to be in our shoes.'

Tracey Crouch MP

Preface

THIS BOOK'S premise is simple. If I take my wife to a film I know inside out, but which she is not familiar with, I look forward to her opinions on the characters, story arc and plot twists. If I take her to my favourite restaurant, which I visited before we met, I listen to her opinions on the flavour combinations, freshness and value for money of the dishes I ordered. But, if we go to a game of football that involves 22 men chasing a bag of air around, in the hope of depositing it in two sets of plastic netting, this is too profound a concept for her female brain to process.

Let's just give that insanity time to breathe. Karen spends her working life managing challenging and demanding groups and comes home to three children (one of them aged 54) who need her care. But the profound nuances of 'boot it long' or 'kick it into row Z' (yes, I watch League Two) must be kept from her, like Robbie Savage and a blow-dryer.

Or, as Sky Sports presenter Laura Woods so eloquently expressed in her late January 2022 tweet: 'What is it about football that people can't accept something if it's coming out of a woman's mouth? Women can be brain surgeons. They can save your life. They can go to the moon. But they can't give you an opinion about football. It's bonkers.'

This book doesn't slot home the open goal of how poorly men often treat women in football. Instead, it is a strident call to arms for both genders to seize the momentum created by Her Game Too (HGT), Women in Football and a cavalry of other empowering campaigners to create real change for a meaningfully inclusive game. A range of inspirational, empowering female voices and supportive male ones plot out a manifesto for a football future that repels the hydra of Project Big Picture, the Super Franchise and its next incarnation that is slithering towards a game inspiring all the jeopardy of a Ligue 1 title race.

Talking of which, what is wrong with so many of us men? The vast majority of us love and respect our mums, girlfriends, wives, sisters, nieces and grans. We know they have overcome indifference at best and misogyny at worst to raise families, run countries and right wrongs. But there remain too many of us wearing our Y-fronted chromosomes as a badge of blind pride. This is what baffles me. If you are a racist, you hate everything about someone who looks different to you in your misguided belief in your superiority. The same goes for homophobes who demonise people with different orientations into cartoonish urban legends hellbent on tearing down society's fabric through their natural behaviour. So, if most men have respect for women, why do so many male football fans act in such boorish and brainless ways?

***

Formed by Caz May and Lucy Ford on 15 May 2021 (FA Cup Final day of course!), HGT has always taken a front-foot approach to call out the misogynistic views of dinosaurs like Richard Keys and Mark Clattenburg.

In this book, I look back in awe at their huge progress so far and listen to Caz, Lucy and the rest of the redoubtable dozen founders as they project forward to challenges that remain if football is to be truly inclusive, taking on the repellent behaviour football's custodians have let slide for far too long. We try to work out why so many men seem threatened by a female perspective and profile and plot out a pathway to a brighter future for all football fans.

A Game of Two Halfwits commiserates a decade since former Sky Sports presenters Gray and Keys showed us in sharp relief what women (not ladies) in football are fighting against. We also celebrate the Premier League of Pathfinders which prepared the ground for Caz, Lucy and the HGT crew.

I then listen to why Her Game Too is so important, why it has had such a massive impact on the game in such a short space of time and how it supports other incredibly successful female empowerment movements like Women in Football. HGT's influence and soft power are also creating an unstoppable momentum demanding tangible change in football that is now being heard in Premier League clubs after their partnerships with Everton, Leeds United and Brentford. Surely, when Caz and Lucy started, they would never have thought that George Best's son would have been inspired by them to become a women's football club chairman at Dorking FC.

> *'Women don't want to stand out from the crowd, we want to belong to it.'*
>
> Caoimhe O'Neill
> *The Athletic*

Our Manifesto for Change coalesces around the HGT mission statement that is both a rallying cry and an antidote to the 1921 FA travesty of banning women's football for half a century after:

> *'Complaints having been made as to football being played by women, Council felt impelled to express the strong opinion that the game of football is quite unsuitable for females and should not be encouraged.'*

A century later, HGT provides the perfect response to this dismissive thinking:

> *'Here at Her Game Too, we are a group of 12*
> *women who are passionate about football and*
> *working to eradicate sexism in the football*
> *industry. We want women and girls of all ages*
> *to feel confident and safe sharing their opinion*
> *about football both online and in real life*
> *without fear of sexist abuse.'*

Her Game Too plots out a vibrant, powerful manifesto for change driven by this pride of lionesses whose unstoppable force will not be restricted by back channelling, lobbying or red tape. All hail the HGT squad and those who join them on their journey of inclusive enlightenment for a game desperately in need of their drive, energy, and determination.

> *We cannot change the past*
> *But we can shape the future.*

About the Author

SO WHY is a man writing a book about women's football? There are obvious reasons for challenging the stereotypes and prejudices towards the women's game propagated by people I share a chromosome with, but it is also something very different. Previously, I lived in Bangkok, I remember my first game at the ramshackle local club Muang Thong United, where a couple of hundred fans gathered in the only stand at the 'stadium'. Within minutes (helped by the oceans of rough local beer) I was hooked and became a born-again advocate of Thai football to friends and work colleagues. Their responses ranged from apathy to ridicule. Why bother watching Thai football when the English Premier League was pumped relentlessly (and illegally) through every roadside bar TV screen?

Despite its challenges, Thai football was to take off to such an extent that huge stadiums were built, crowds grew rapidly and players who would come four on a moped to training now cruised up in sportscars. It felt like I had ownership of the increasing popularity of Thai football by being one of the early adopters, and this must be how women in football feel. The pushback and barriers to entry bond you tightly with fellow fans as you fight against behemoths intent on hoovering up every 'customer' in their orbit. But you can take a stand and say you believe differently as haters clicking keyboards in their mother's back bedrooms spew their bile and secretly wish they had your passion.

I love football. Too often this phrase is glossed over or considered the childish response of an emotionally stunted fan. But football goes DNA deep. Not only does it span family generations but, like real love should, motivates us to ridiculous flights of fancy. Saturday, 25 September 2021's Villa victory at Old Trafford, the first since 2009, made any titbit of detail fair game. However poor the YouTube video or asinine the article, everything had to be consumed in a glorious day of freestyle emotional catharsis. As Keiran Maguire says in his and Kevin Day's imperious pod *The Price of Football*, 'it is the first thing we think about when we wake up and the last thing we think about before we go to bed'. This sounds ridiculous only to those who can't feel real love, because football love is one of the world's few limitless resources. My all-consuming football affair does not mean I feel any less towards my wife or (occasionally) my sons. It is not sordid (my wife noticed my profession of love on Facebook for Villa's keeper Emi Martinez and shrugged. It may have been a different reaction if that comment had been directed at my next-door neighbour).

Former Women in Football CEO Jane Purdon describes the 'happy madness' football commands in the excellent anthology *Football, She Wrote*.[1] Describing the moment in 1973 when the unfancied Sunderland scored against an imperious Leeds United in that season's FA Cup Final, 33 minutes into the game, she says:

'Let me tell you how my seven-year-old heart experienced this. At 3.33pm and 50 seconds, I was a child who observed football with curiosity. Then, for a split second, there was just me and Ian Porterfield. Then he did this thing. And then I felt myself falling into a deep, deep pit. That pit was love. At

---

1 Authors various, *Football, She Wrote: An Anthology of Women's Writing on the Game* p.172, (Floodlit Dreams. Kindle Edition).

3.33pm and 52 seconds, my heart had gone forever. I was a football fan and a Sunderland fan.'

***

Football love also allows us to keep a mistress. I am a lifelong Villa fan now living in Devon, and a season-ticket holder at Exeter City. It doesn't make me feel like a football swinger (Kevin Day may disagree), just a fan with lots of love (and frustration) to give. Most importantly in the context of this book, football love is not limited to who can feel it. On the terraces of my local Bangkok club and the away game Happy Bus, where free rough-as-guts Leo beer provided by the club meant games were often hazy or non-recollections, we were male, female, young, old, gay, or straight but always Muang Thong United.

I was working in a sensible and reliable job as the head of marketing and public relations for Harrow School Bangkok, but I walked away from it to dive head first into the crazy world of Thai Football (there's a book in there somewhere). Financially ruinous but filled with lifelong memories, the whole experience held heady and magnetic insanity that, five years later, is still slowly sinking in. The access it gave me to the power brokers with limitless funds was both intoxicating and occasionally terrifying. I wouldn't have changed a thing, even if my bank manager strongly disagrees.

1

The Euros. Don't Watch Women's Football

YOU MAY have heard. There was a football tournament in England this summer. The England team took on and beat all comers through irrepressible force (Norway) sheer guts and determination against a technically gifted and tactically advanced Spain (until their coach's bizarre substitution decisions) and showed how far their game has advanced when dismantling a largely amateur Northern Ireland. Plenty about that final to come ... Stadiums have been packed, television audiences have smashed records (for that England and Spain game it peaked at 7.6 million plus 1.5 million BBC streams) and games often full of technical and physical mastery have described dramatic and compelling story arcs. There were 9.3 million BBC viewers and two million streams for the semi final meant record keepers were updating faster than those cat furiously typing memes. So here I am 100 words into the paragraph and I only mentioned the 'w' of wins and not of 'women' Why? I never watch women's football. I watch the beautiful game played by artists like De Bryne or Bronze, defensive titans like Bright or Van Dijk and daydream achievers like Kane or Stanway.

Now with the broadest of platforms, increasing seasons of elite training and financial security in their legs, lungs and minds, the hype comes from the contest (and THAT backheel) instead of being fuelled by hope. When alking to *The Athletic*'s Sarah Shephard in July 2022, consummate presenter Gabby Logan admitted that had been previously, especially for the 2007 World Cup in China, it had been a challenge, 'being really enthusiastic about something but knowing that it's not quite there yet'. The Euros have been a case study in 'build it and they will come'. Not only is the product on offer now consistently of the highest quality, but there was reassuring normality walking into our local pub with all the screens showing Germany beating Austria. Drinkers ridiculed Austrian keeper Manuela Zinsberger for gifting the Germans a second goal because of her decision-making rather than chromosome count, which lowers the temperature of conversations and creates normality in evaluating the action over the actors.

FIFA 23. Don't Play Women's Football

The next FIFA iteration expands to include the WSL and French Division 1 Féminine for the first time. The game's cover features two players, Kylian Mbappé and Sam Kerr, and also adds the Women's World Cup in Australia and New Zealand. To be fair to EA Sport, women have been included since 2015, but with only a smattering of international sides and, in FIFA 22, the profile had evolved to include 17 international squads and increasing access to features like Pro Club modes allowing thumb twiddlers to create a female player. Previous efforts invited talk of gender tokenism, but FIFA 23 (the 30th and final edition created by EA Sport) should help lay that to rest. Like so many of the issues surrounding the women's game, success will come when no one (apart from apoplectic keyboard warriors) even notices their player or team's gender and focusses their ire on poor defending or missed open goals.

Euro 2022. Don't Ruin Women's Football

In his predictably eviscerating and affirming article on 18 July 18th John Nicholson described this tournament as, 'like a filter for the dickheads who spoil football for the rest of us'. Echoing a phrase Boris Johnson used to berate Putin (sorry to drag him in, John), the 'toxic masculinity' that often blights our matchday experiences drives the atmosphere down to the lowest common denominator of a drink/drug-fuelled bear pit where the 'it's only banter' defence is trotted out for a range of reprehensible behaviours. Railing against what he sees as a world becoming more conflicted and confrontational, Nicholson sees the women's game as an instructive inversion of these testosterone-fuelled trends.

The inclusive, welcoming and supportive atmosphere we feel at Exeter City Women FC is a window into the women's game and fuels the Euros. Free from boorish and belligerent posturing, Euros crowds also reminded me of my time working in Thai football where families would see games as a chance to enjoy each other's company, knowing they were safe from having to explain to granny what a 'pedo' was or why we are all encouraged to 'shit on the City'.

Nicholson's key point is punishingly telling. The overwhelming dominance of men in general and a particular male demographic in particular feeds on itself with a race to the bottom of general unpleasantness cloaked in the lie that this is what real support looks like. The Euros crowds had a balance: of age, gender and orientation so that abuse has no room to breathe, fester and explode like some inky boil but is stifled at source. Nicholson draws a powerful image of those who prefer male dominance and a carte blanche for cretins, describing those who feel he is a woolly 'woke' bleeding heart liberal as watching on with:

'faces angrily twisted like an inflamed hernia, indignant that someone is neutering their desire to piss in gardens and insert flaming objects into their rectum'.

It used to be a simple logic about the women's game that, with so few fans watching, the mob didn't get a chance to rule. But, with its exponential growth, the women's game has not switched off its 'dickhead filter' and Nicholson's article climaxes with the sadness this joyous new footballing world has engendered in the men hell-bent on dumb weekend behaviour. We could have had this in the men's game. In Thailand, crowd violence is often driven by politics, but when Granny sits next to you and your daughter is on your knee, the civilising power of women creates a welcoming and intoxicating atmosphere (especially after sampling the local Thai beers). Gabby Logan describes women's football to *The Athletic*'s Sarah Shephard as 'a beautiful evolution to watch' that mirrors the world we live in, or aspire to. 'Football reflects so many attitudes in society. Sometimes I think it reflects where we are as a civilisation in terms of attitudes and how important subjects like racism and homophobia are handled. If football treats it seriously then it sends a really strong message. That's why the women's game being so much more professional is really important in terms of women's sport generally and women's access to things they want to do in society.'

Be My Plus One

The path to parity may feel dauntingly long, but there is a fiendishly simple and massive step we can all make. When we go to our next Exeter City Women or Larkhall Athletic, Chelsea or Aston Villa game just bring one other person with you. Clubs could give the plus ones a free single, double or treble match voucher to thank them and, like a cheap Ryanair ticket where an empty seat is replaced by a customer open to purchase, food, merchandise or matchday programmes can help boost coffers and build atmospheres.

With the women's season around the corner, each league can, like EFL website templates, corporately and consistently encourage fans to bring a friend and share their experiences, with regular reminders built into their online messages. Lionesses promoting lower-level clubs they started with could reflect Alessia Russo's decision to give her shirt to young fan Nancy Richardson after she held up a sign to the queen of backheels highlighting the team both of them played for:

'Russo I play at Bearsted, please can I have your shirt?'

I admit my club bias, but I strongly feel that building from the bottom up is the key here. The much-mentioned 'football pyramid' cannot survive if the disparity between the Lioness legends and those in the third and fourth tiers is allowed to become an unbridgeable gap. Coventry United, that I talk about later, are the red flags that warn us not to tread the risky financial path many of the lower league men's teams have taken but to pursue a culture of fan-driven inclusivity driving universal growth over top-heavy conspicuous spending.

So look around your family, friendship groups and neighbourhoods and, as a famous philosopher didn't say:

'The journey of a thousand fans begins with a single text'.

Ode to Joy

As a lecturer in marketing, I'm jealous of Leigh Moore who, when moving from his marketing role at the FA in 2012, coined the term 'Lionesses'. No more clunky stumbling sentences. A clean, resonating brand was born that needed no explanation or qualification. And that brand is, in the words of The Greeter's Guild's Troy Hawke, 'smashing it'.

So to the final. Where to start? When the game kicked off, how about the matchday programme on the Amazon Hot New Release chart at number four (above *The Football Yearbook* and The Zlatan's autobiography)? Or a crowd of 87,192: a record for a Euros final (men or women). Maybe the 101 new grassroots girls and women's teams created by a single tournament sponsor? The data is dazzling but, as heady as these figures are, there is something more profound at play here. It feels like the game has, finally, grown up. Instead of being an increasingly unsustainable echo chamber of stale ideas, joy has smashed down barriers built up over centuries by male, pale and stale cartels closing their minds to half the population. There was just time for Caz and Lucy to meet up with England legend Sue Smith (who wore a Her Game Too badge for the day) before diving into the infectious, rambunctious, life-affirming joy that climaxed on 31 July 2022.

Like life, football is a perpetual pursuit of fleeting perfection. But that Sunday afternoon served up all the elements of joy to keep these dark days of Russian bombs and rising bills at bay. The game was officiated by Ukrainian Kateryna Monzul four months after she'd fled her home in Kharkiv and lived underground at her parents' house for five days before making the arduous journey across Europe to take shelter in Germany; her nationality and story resonated, but she was here on merit. Just like our lionesses. Playing with an outsized Her Game Too flag positioned behind one of the Wembley goals was validation of the hard yards my HGT legends have volunteered in the face of bitter jealousy from a foetid male minority. But, once the festival of joy was given full freedom, it was time for calm concentration and to write the tournament's conclusion.

The game was the story of women's football. Nerve-shredding moments that flirted with failure but, ultimately, basked in glorious success. Despite going behind and losing their talismanic striker Alexandra Popp to injury in the warm-up, Germany purred with finely honed precision as they explored fault lines in the English defence. After a dominant second half, they found their moment and, with 11 minutes left, carved out a beautiful goal worthy of their stunning style. Only 11 heads remained unbowed but then, after 111 sapping minutes, Chloe Kelly pounced on a moment of fortune in the German box to calmly poke home a goal that will resonate through generations. That moment transformed women's football from the back page to the front page and meant it can now turn a new page. Among the legion of content, this joke summed up what the women had done:

'Men:

Football's coming home!! It's coming home!! It's coming!!

Women, 60yrs later: ... FFS I'll get it myself.'

Alex Scott, who has seen first-hand the evolution of the beautiful women's game, struck the perfect tone for those suddenly deciding that women's football is worthy of their attention:

'We begged so many people to back us, and they weren't brave enough. I'm not standing up at corporate events any more begging people to get involved in the women's game. You know what? If you're not involved, you missed the train. We left the station without you.'

What heightens the intensity of this glorious kaleidoscope of community is how this represents nothing more than the end of the beginning. Let me tell you more ...

2.

Happy Birthday Her Game Too!

FROM TODAY, FA Cup Finals have an added layer of pride. Each one represents a Her Game Too anniversary. Saturday, 14 May also happened to be my deadline for this book so, for the final time, I caught up with Caz, Lucy and the HGT legends to reflect on their astonishing progress as we all travelled up to Birmingham to celebrate an incredible year at the stylish Gosta Green bar. The scale of the campaign was clear from the number of guests that Calum Best was hosting and from the fact that the party was sponsored by High Street brands Nationwide Building Society and Jewson. The increasing influence of the HGT message had been clear on 21 January when Caz appeared on Sky Sports' *Inside the WSL* to share the Her Game Too story, but also project some of the short-, medium- and long-term aims of the campaign. Reflecting on how their viral post was second trending within a day of the FA Cup Final itself as they racked up a million hits in the first 24 hours, the support of key female voices like Laura Woods and Michelle Owen and an increasing number of male footballers showing their support, the growth in momentum was headily exponential. In conversation with presenter Jessica Creighton, Caz also mapped out how the future could look when she explained what the campaign's ultimate goal was:

'To see more young girls being inspired to play football, to watch football, to work in football in terms of being a physio for example. I want to see more girls stay in colleges. That's why we want to do work with colleges. We want to get them inspired and encouraged to go into that sort of role and for them not to have to face the fear of facing misogynistic comments. Obviously, it's a lot of work to do because it's going to take some time and it's going to take a lot of educating to do that, but if we can get these modules into schools and start from a young age then maybe we can start encouraging and inspiring young girls to get into it.'

Making the Case for Safe Space

The day started with a welcome speech by Calum, a man whose restored purpose I describe later in the book as a case study of the good HGT are doing globally and personally. Then it was down to business with the FA Cup Final beamed around the Gosta Green screens. As the event was invitation only, everyone we met had helped shape the Her Game Too story. And what a story it was. People had come from all over the country to be part of an event showcasing the very best of us all, supported by proud parents, partners and friends.

It was also the setting to unveil the campaign's next innovation. This venue was selected as the first of 500 proposed pubs described by Calum as committed to making watching football more welcoming for women and girls. The energy, passion and commitment made the evening thrum, nicely fuelled by the free food and drink from our sponsors represented by the highly supportive figure of Chis Hull. As we all bade our farewells and dispersed into a balmy Brummy May evening, the overriding feeling was of leaving an arena of common purpose recharged, (heavily) refuelled and doubly determined to share the message driving the HGT heartbeat. We love football. Full stop. End of story.

3.

The Big Bang Moment

ONLY TWO weeks before needing to send this book off
to the editor, the kind of 'big bang moment' happened that
just left us all gobsmacked. For those who struggle to sleep,
parliamentlive.tv is normally the perfect way to get you
snoring in seconds. But not on 25 April 2022. During the
Government response to the Fan-Led Review of Football,
Karin Smyth, the Labour MP for Bristol South may have
slightly misread HGT as a Gashead (strong sense of loyalty)
campaign, but Lucy and Caz were name-dropped in the
House of Commons!

'Rivalry in the city is very intense, but can I draw the
Right Honourable Minister's attention to supporting the work
of Caz May and Lucy Ford, the founders of Bristol Rovers'
Her Game Too and can I press him a bit on the details of the
review on women's football and hope that the work of Her
Game Too and all the women and girls involved in grassroots
football is included in that review.'

But this stunning spike in profile only served to
underscore the size of the task that still remains.

To illustrate the enormity of the challenge, step forward
Kenny Shiels. Gobsmackingly, in April 2022 after his
Northern Ireland team had been soundly beaten by England,
their coach shared with the post-match press how: 'Girls and

women are more emotional than men. So, they take a goal going in not very well.'

Failing to read the increasingly stunned room, he picked his spade and kept digging.

'I'm sure you will have noticed if you go through the patterns – when a team concedes a goal, they concede a second one in a very, very short space of time. [It happens] right through the whole spectrum of the women's game, because girls and women are more emotional than men. So, they take a goal going in not very well.'

The only sign of self-awareness came at the very end when, scanning the incredulous room of journalists seeing their story rising through the editorial ranks, he decided to summarise his career epitaph: 'I shouldn't have told you that.'

Really? Do you think? Luckily, the football world had already moved on and even the closed-loop world of the Premier League was waking up to the need for Her Game Too.

*****

On Boxing Day 2021, as we woke up woozy, the best possible news began to help clear our heads at 10am, when Her Game Too made a stunning announcement. Those of us who had followed their progress knew they were an unstoppable force, but the Premier League often followed a different tune to the clubs below. Not anymore. Everton are a club of firsts. First to be presented with the league championship trophy, to wear numbered shirts, and to use dugouts and goal nets, they had now become the first Premier League club to form an official partnership with Her Game Too. Despite a highly challenging season, Everton were the perfect choice of all the Premier League members to smash through the glass ceiling, with their highly respected CEO leading the charge.

Known as 'Prof' to her colleagues, Professor Denise Barrett-Baxendale MBE is the CEO of Everton and one of the most high-profile women in football. With more than a decade at the Toffees, she knows the club inside out and is focussing on her remit of working closely with the local community. The Everton in The Community initiative has gone from strength to strength under her stewardship. Internationally recognised and the winner of a century of local, national and international awards, it shows Denise is a team player who looks out for the club and community. The MBE she received in 2014 was for her services to Merseyside. During the Covid pandemic, Denise and her team were given a Gold award at 2021's Football Business Awards for their response to the crisis. In a swift and focussed campaign, she oversaw 20,000 checks and welfare phone calls, the delivery of 17,000 emergency food parcels and the delivery of 300,000 meals for school children. If you need help in a crisis, Denise is the person you want with you.

There is also a poignant and poetic symmetry to the timing of Everton's decision. As I recount in chapter, 4 Born Out of Time: The Ballad of Lily Parr, huge Goodison Park crowds watched women's football before the misogynists at the FA banned them in 1921. There were few bigger games than the one played that a year ago in front of 53,000 fans. The synergy between the values of Her Game Too and the People's Club also gives great credit to both sides of the partnership. It will join other initiatives under the umbrella campaign of 'All Together Now', which for three years, has been highlighting and challenging some of the poor treatment faced by women at matches. Everton Women are also the only team (at the time of writing) in the WSL to play at a purpose-built football stadium, showing the club's heartfelt commitment to supporting the whole game.

Joint founder of Her Game Too, Lucy Ford was justifiably proud and humbled by the latest chapter being written for her campaign:

'This is a major milestone for us and our campaign to have a club the size of Everton supporting us. The poignant date of the announcement is also special to us as on this day 101 years ago Goodison Park played host to one of the most seminal women's games in history.'

A new milestone would be created only a few weeks later when, on 3 March, the 100th professional, semi-professional and grassroots partner club signed up. An astonishing achievement.

When the official Everton Twitter account shared the news of their partnership with their 2.6 million followers, the response was overwhelmingly supportive, with comments like @connor_t94's 'Incredible step in the right direction for the team at @HerGameToo #HerGameToo massive steps this' and Caz's beloved Bristol Rovers Women's @GasGirlsWFC with 'superb news for our friends at @HerGameToo! Amazing to see the campaign going from strength to strength.'

But dispiritingly and illustrative of why Her Game Too needs our full support were comments from a small minority of the mindless. For @DavidFo38145364 it was an example of 'more woke nonsense' and @RCharlton1966 sputtering into his keyboard tucked away in his mother's back bedroom, gave us 'what next? Can't I just go to a bloody football match without political messages being rammed down my throat? Christ.' The beauty of the comments is that the heartfelt support will encourage more Premier League clubs to sign up, and the apoplectic brain donors' responses will have exactly the same effect.

In conversation with Talksport's Bradley Hayden on 7 January, Everton's Izzy Christiansen gave wholehearted and enthusiastic backing to their Her Game Too partnership.

'[Her Game Too is] integral in terms of highlighting the role that women play in football. I think it's great that the campaign has been formed by fans because it comes from the heart and they are genuine feelings towards being a female fan in football and how it's impacted them over the years.

'It's great that Everton have decided to get on board and officially become a supporting partner of Her Game Too. It shows the diversity within the club as a whole and I think it's a great partnership.'

***

This breakthrough gives Caz, Lucy and the team a much bigger platform to show and a louder megaphone to share the message of how to address sexist attitudes in the game. It also gives an added sense of momentum and profile to all the clubs already signed up from the Championship down through the professional and amateur leagues. Her Game Too have established and developed a huge range of innovative, hard-hitting and creative campaigns, but now they will also be able to tap into a high-profile and professionally driven marketing power, overseen by a widely respected woman at the top of her game.

In early January 2022, members of the Everton fans forum Siobhan Doran and Jazz Bal stood pitch-side at Goodison Park to celebrate their HGT partnership. This must have been a surreal watch for the HGT crew, less than a year after they started a campaign from scratch.

This huge breakthrough was followed up by Leeds United on 17 February 2022. Their newly agreed partnership with HGT was showcased three days later with the arrival of Manchester United to Elland Road. The players promoted this stunningly successful campaign during their warm-ups after two first-team stars Kalvin Phillips and Raphinha had posed in Her Game Too shirts with one of the founders and an avid Leeds fan Jessica Furness, on the day of the agreement. These shirts were worn in the warm-ups and the campaign was promoted in the match-day programme and on big screens around the stadium.

Talking to Leeds Live's Beren Cross, United's CEO Angus Kinnear said: 'We are really pleased to finally announce our new partnership with Her Game Too, as we continue to fight against any form of discrimination.

'Sexism and abuse towards females will absolutely not be tolerated by anyone associated with the club and we hope that by supporting important campaigns and organisations such as Her Game Too, it will only help us in ensuring that everyone feels welcome and safe when they are at Elland Road.

'I know all of our supporters will get behind this campaign and help us to encourage women and girls to attend games, show their support freely online and follow the club they love.'

Jessica, when talking to the club, was understandably elated with the new partnership: 'As the co-founder and Leeds United ambassador of Her Game Too, this partnership means the world to me! It was always a personal aim of mine to see this happen since we started the campaign last year. Football is most certainly a game for all but sadly sexism is still rife in the beautiful game.

'Since a young age I've been a hugely passionate Leeds fan but have always felt out of place as a female in a male-dominated game. I'm really looking forward to working with the club on promoting equality, raising awareness on sexism and empowering women in football. We want to make their experiences as enjoyable and safe as possible, not just for the female Leeds fans of today but also tomorrow.

'The club have been amazing and so eager with getting this partnership over the line in the best way possible from start to finish and I am so grateful for that. I can't wait to see what we can achieve together. Marching on together, no matter what gender you are – it's Her Game Too.'

***

By the end of February 2022, the decision by Brentford to wear Her Game Too warm-up shirts for their game against

Newcastle meant that, in the space of days, Kalvin Phillips and Christian Eriksen had happily worn and shared photos of themselves wearing the HGT t-shirts with their huge online following. This was truly mind blowing. The profile for HGT in the match-day programmes (the Leeds United copy featuring a pencil-drawn image of their number five Robin Kock next to the Her Game Too logo was particularly captivating) also created a permanent record of the agreements. Brentford chose a historic day to publicly team-up with HGT, as it marked the return to football of Eriksen after his shocking collapse in Denmark's opening Euro 2020 game against Finland. The stars had aligned.

***

If these were Her Game Too's Premier League 'big bang' moments then, on 22 February 2022, they made another huge step towards being a truly global brand. On the same day, Czech-based Prague Raptors FC and American College Soccer Placement Experts SRUSA Women's Soccer signed to join 42 professional football clubs (at the time) across the UK already partnered with the campaign. This was supported the following week when Her Game Too USA opened a parallel campaign to its British namesake.

Now there was real momentum, profile and good will from Premier League clubs to join a truly global movement. On 27 April 2022, Wolves announced their partnership with HGT. Their first sentence felt significant and appropriate. Less than a year before starting the campaign, a major English team would write, 'Wolves join a number of EFL clubs in committing to the cause'. Her Game Too materials were to be given high profile around Molineux and in match-day programmes.

The whole process also underscored the important role the HGT ambassadors and advocates play in not only making first contact with clubs, but negotiating good will toward a mutually beneficial conclusion. Georgina Slawinski did the hard yards both as HGT ambassador and a health engagement officer at Wolves Foundation. She shared with her club how: 'At Wolves Foundation, we recognise the power that football has to motivate, educate and inspire local people and communities across Wolverhampton to change their lives for the better. We are all really looking forward to working closely with Wolves and Her Game Too to make a positive impact for women in football.'

News of Bournemouth's promotion being sealed after their stunning late win over Nottingham Forest on 3 May 2022 meant the Cherries joined the ever-expanding group of Premier League clubs partnered with Her Game Too. Astonishing.

***

On 15 May Aston Villa joined the ranks of high-profile clubs making a strong commitment to this outstanding campaign when their Villa Bellas joined up and they even created their own piece of HGT history. For the first time, the chosen club ambassadors were all players. Lena, Priyanka and Sarah all had unique insights to offer ways of bringing together the club, fans and local claret and blue community. Then, on 26 May, the Villa men's team also committed to partnering with the HGT legends. But, as the football season concluded (and what a finish it was for Bristol Rovers and the ever-growing Her Game Too Premier League clubs who maintained their top-flight status), the HGT team took a break to recharge their batteries, surely? Not a bit of it. On 24 May 2022, both Gloucestershire County Cricket Club and their women's team Western Storm became the world's first cricket clubs to partner with HGT. The club press release put their commitment across with a funky acrostic that explained how they would:

Create strong relationships with Clubs, Trusts, and Foundations

Research and recognise cricket-specific issues

Improve the presence at cricket grounds to build a more welcoming environment for young girls and women

Continue to campaign against sexism and online abuse in cricket

Keep championing women within cricket (players, staff, AND fans)

Educate around equality throughout the game

To create a strong sense of community.

Caz, in her usual indefatigable way, was delighted to enter a new arena of sporting respect. She told the club:

'We have some great ambassadors for cricket on our team already, who can work with Gloucestershire Cricket to drive this forward and begin making a change in the world of cricket. We would like to thank Glos for this opportunity and for becoming the first cricket team to take this vital step in supporting #HerGameToo.'

4

In Conversation with Her Game Too Founders Caz and Lucy

I FIRST caught up with Caz May the day after her amazing experience at Wembley on 12 October 2021 (not because of the match, unfortunately) where she and Lucy Ford had been guests of honour at England's World Cup qualifier against Hungary.

Matt: 'Caz, tell us about last night at Wembley. Looking at the photos, it looks like you had an amazing time.'

Caz: 'We did! We were invited to it because Chris Hull, who is the Nationwide Respect Ambassador and works for Sky Sports asked us. He was really keen to support the campaign and he invited us along yesterday so that we could meet more people to talk about it and see if there is anything we can do with the FA's Nationwide Mutual Respect Campaign. It was all off the back of that, which is amazing. We had a really positive chat with Jimmy Bullard last night too and Fenners from Soccer AM, David James as well, who are all really keen to support us.'

Matt: 'I noticed on your website something called Club 92. Can you tell me a little bit more about that?'

Caz: 'It's a little project we started where we want to champion a girl from every single club, whether it's a diehard fan, member of staff, physio, and we'll put her on the website.

It's a little challenge that we've set ourselves for them to talk about why they love football or why they got into doing what they do, and we want to tick off every single club.'

Matt: 'What are the key areas you are trying to get out there for Her Game Too?'

Caz: 'Educating is quite a big thing for us, so what we want to do eventually is get modules into schools. What we can do is work with community trusts of football clubs that we are partnered with because they go to schools anyway as part of their normal routine. A lot of the comments we've had are from parents that have young girls that have been told on the playground that they can't join in because it's a man's game, which is quite concerning that actually it is something that is ingrained into young minds still, so that's something we want to start educating about at a young age. Also, in school, there are rarely any girls' teams available. It's always the boys that play football and the girls play netball so we are pushing forward to that equal opportunity for both sexes.

'The other key area for us is about a safe environment at football, so what we've done with the 20 clubs that we've partnered with so far is that we've got them to put a system in place but also make a pledge against sexist abuse and they need to educate their staff and their stewards to say we need to stamp it out. On the back of that, we have got them to set up a reporting system. So, Exeter City have a text messaging service, Rovers have got a hotline you can call. Some clubs have an email you can send where your seat number was, and some clubs just ask fans to report to stewards.

'So, it's about having that in place and having posters around the stadium to say this is what you do if you encounter this. So, it's letting female fans know that they are supported, they are welcome. If they have any trouble, then it won't be tolerated, and this is where you go.'

***

As Caz reflected on the first few months of running Her Game Too, she summarised the highs and lows of standing up for what you believe in and the sacrifices needed to keep going in the face of pushback and abuse, in this tweet, posted on 13 October 2021, after she and Lucy had been invited to be VIP guests at Wembley Stadium: 'Starting up #HerGameToo has been both wonderful and stressful. Almost five months of working alongside a full-time job and on the receiving end of online bullying & trolling… days like yesterday where you feel appreciated makes it all worth it.'

***

Caz drew breath on 11 January 2022 to give me an update on the campaign's stellar success, saying: 'It's fair to say that things have well and truly taken off in the past seven months since myself and 11 other female football fans spoke out about our experiences of sexism in football. It feels like the campaign has been going a lot longer than just seven months.

'I look back to when I first considered it, when I felt at my lowest after falling victim to a Twitter pile-on that resulted in a barrage of misogynistic insults towards me and little to do with the actual football. No one could have convinced my disheartened self that less than a year down the line, I would have stood up to these trolls by sparking a nationwide campaign to tackle sexism in football and helping other women to feel safe and secure at games. But I did that – and #HerGameToo is thriving.'

Caz looked back at the idea behind the campaign, its launch, and then summarised the first seven months of work.

'Back to the beginning … I'm always someone who strives to turn a negative into a positive. When I found myself feeling like I couldn't go back to football out of fear, that's when I knew something had to change. No one should feel this way and we all deserve to feel safe at stadiums, particularly at our home club. Sexism isn't the only form of discrimination – we have some great movements such as Kick it Out and Rainbow Laces that are tackling racism and homophobia. It's time to add sexism under that umbrella and I knew I could use my personal experience as a fan to help raise awareness of the issue.

'This was always something I couldn't tackle on my own. I knew there would be plenty of girls I could get on board who have experiences similar to what I have. I only needed to scroll down Twitter for five minutes on some days before seeing that another woman had been subjected to sexist abuse online.

'I saw several tweets and it helped me to collate a list of strong, outspoken women to be the original faces of the campaign.

'I had ten passionate girls nailed down for the original launch. Lucy, Leah, Eve, Jess, Bobbi, Abbie, Emily, Hollie, Izzy and Caitlin. I was almost settled on those ten until I came across Amy Clement on my news feed, speaking out about the sexist abuse she received for her football opinions. The abuse she received and still does receive is some of the worst I've seen. It was a no-brainer to reach out and ask if she wanted to be a part of our new campaign.

'The group chat was set up on 6 May – nine days before we launched the campaign video. Those nine days were busy. We wanted to get it right as we only had one chance at it. We needed a strong name for the campaign and we were back and forth with ideas before settling on #HerGameToo. The 'too' is so important to us. This isn't a campaign to take over – we want to stand WITH men. We want to be a part of football and feel welcomed. Let's all support the club together, as one, without any discrimination towards others.

'The launch, on 15 May 2021 ... We were unsure of the best day to launch the campaign. It needed to be impactful and timing was crucial. We considered perhaps during the Euros or at the start of the 21/22 season. It was only when the BBC released an article on sexist abuse within football that we realised the time was now. It was such a hot topic and we wanted to capitalise on that. We teased the idea of #HerGameToo on our social channels before launching the campaign video at 10am on FA Cup Final day.

'I remember staying up late on 14 May, finalising and tweaking the campaign video. I also spent time setting up the @hergametoo social accounts to make sure we were ready. I was a mixture of excited and nervous. I had no idea what the reaction was going to be and if we were even going to be taken seriously. It was at this moment, that I was glad I wasn't doing this on my own ...

'On Saturday, 15 May at 10am it was posted and out there. The immediate response was incredible. Within one minute we had 100 retweets and my phone wouldn't stop buzzing. It was seriously amazing to see the support flooding in and just how many women felt like they could resonate with us. We gained 6,000 followers on the Twitter page and hit one million views within the first 24 hours of launching. We also received tweets of support from several professional football clubs, the EFL and from women we look up to, such as Laura Woods and Michelle Owen. It was an overwhelming 24 hours. We are so grateful to everyone who supported and shared.

'How it's going ... seven months since the launch and it has been fairly non-stop. We get dozens of emails and messages a day. Many of our evenings and lunch hours are spent in Her Game Too meetings. We all work full-time, so in order to keep the fire burning for Her Game Too we have to work around those hours. It can be tiring and I've had many meltdowns but what we have achieved so far is so rewarding. I wouldn't change it for the world.

'One of our biggest achievements to date is getting the recognition and support from Everton. They announced our partnership on Boxing Day – which was the 101st anniversary of the ladies' fixture at Goodison Park that attracted a crowd of more than 53,000. With this back story, it was so fitting that Everton became our first Premier League club partnership.

'We know there are a few people out there who don't like what we are doing. We have had many abusive messages off the back of launching this campaign – but the positivity always outweighs the negativity. Despite the trolls, we will keep fighting the good fight. We have plenty more to come and we are so excited to progress. The support we've had has been so amazing and we thank every single one of you who has supported us. Let's continue to make football a safer space for all and kick out discrimination for good.'

***

On securing club number 19 as Her Game Too partners, Lucy Ford sat down with Roberto Petrucco of the *Sports Gazette* on 27 September 2021. Thanks to him for the permission to reprint this interview.

Roberto Petrucco: 'So obviously the momentum is really growing now there's more clubs coming on. I believe that at Bristol Rovers they've got the logo on the women's kit?'

Lucy: 'Yeah. We are the away kit sponsors for the women's team which was incredible. The Community Trust at Bristol Rovers have gone above and beyond to support us and that was really early on. They came to us and said, "We want to put you on our away kits at no cost to you" which was incredible and I was really fortunate to be part of promoting that and doing the kit launch, which was a really amazing experience for myself. Seeing the shirt, and I mean, I'm biased, because it's Rovers, but it's absolutely beautiful. It's just one of the best shirts I've seen around on men or women.

Roberto: 'So, going back to when it first launched, how long was the process to get the campaign going?

Lucy: 'Caz came to me in April with this idea, but the story really started in January. Obviously, all 12 co-founders and have been watching football for a long time and we've all experienced sexist abuse whether it's online or in person. Caz had a really bad experience in January of this year [2021]. She just tweeted about the scoreline (I think we lost 7-2 to Brentford). She just tweeted laughing because they were losing every week. It was really harmless: it wasn't hurting anyone. It was just a bit of banter. So, the tweet got a lot of retweets and a lot of likes, went viral, but it got on to a lot of people's timelines where they were saying really nasty things like "get back to the kitchen", or "you know nothing about football because you're a woman", saying stuff about her looks and it was just horrendous.

'She said that she literally deleted her Twitter account just because of the sheer amount of abuse that she was getting for just a harmless tweet, like any of us have done. I compare it to when Villa played Liverpool and they won 7-2 and everyone was going on about how Liverpool were rubbish and laughing at them, but no one got someone saying "oh you shouldn't say that". It didn't really get that sort of reaction but for some reason this tweet did, and it was just unacceptable really. Anyway, she said to me how it really affected her mental health.

'So, it was about April then she came to me and she was like, "you know there are these great campaigns for racism and homophobia like Kick It Out? Is there a campaign out there for sexism? A well-known one?" I sat there thinking. I said, "well I don't know of one myself" and she said, "well why don't we do a video? You know, with a few other girls." We'd seen girls that we knew through Twitter talk about their experiences a bit more recently and we thought, "why not do a video highlighting our experiences?" I said, "yes, absolutely". I could picture it straight away, which is kind of how the video came about.

'So, she spoke to the other ten girls asking if they wanted to be a part of it and they all said yes. It was really about three weeks where we got together in Twitter group chats, just kind of discussed some ideas about how we wanted to do it, when we wanted to launch it. The night before we were going to put the video out someone said, "why don't we just do a Twitter, Facebook and Instagram account for it?" We all agreed that was a really good idea and then we could all build up to it on our own Twitter. Someone set it up and we had quite a few followers between us and so we tweeted out saying look out, you know something big is coming at 10am tomorrow and by the time it got to Saturday at 10 o'clock the page on Twitter had got 500 followers, which is pretty decent. So, we tweeted the video at 10 o'clock on Saturday, 15 May, FA Cup Final day and it went viral. I mean to the point that we had amassed a million views on that video on Twitter in 24 hours.

Roberto: 'That's incredible.'

Lucy: 'It was incredible and we were immediately getting support from football clubs, journalists with news articles even in that first 12-to-24-hour period. It was crazy.'

Roberto: 'I actually remember when it launched because I went on my Twitter feed and I obviously follow quite a few football clubs and fans and I was scrolling and saw this same video coming every single time and it was like, "well how long has this been going?" It was amazing how quickly people backed you. Like you said, there are these other kinds of campaigns for equality in different areas but with sexism, there was that gap that's now being kind of filled by yourselves.

'How did you first get a partnership with a club? Was it through Bristol Rovers? How did that all go?'

Lucy: 'Our first big aim was could we get one club to partner with us or one club to put us on their shirt, which meant everything to us because when we set up the campaign I don't think we realised what sort of impact it was going to have and we didn't know how people would react. Bristol Rovers reached out to us as the very first club. Obviously, me and Caz are both Gasheads so we felt really privileged that they were the first Football League club to back us. The men's team and the women's team obviously did it in different ways but still, it meant a lot to us because it showed that the club was really backing the campaign, really believed in our message and really wanted to support it and actually make a difference.

'So, they reached out to us initially and then after that, we thought, "well you know, let's see if there are other clubs out there that want to be a part of this or want to partner with us." We reached out via email and social media seeing if we could find any contacts and just doing it that way. From there, loads of clubs got back in touch with, "yes we really like this" or, "you know this is how we partner". So we were having Zoom calls and Teams calls with the clubs and just talking to them about the ideas and it was really nice chatting to those different people saying how much is needed. Some of them have been female employees.

'Huddersfield have partnered with us now as well and I just thought that's massive. They're a former Premier League club and I was like "Wow, like this is so cool". The supporters' service manager at Huddersfield, Robin, she's been amazing, and she was one of the first people I was in contact with.

'Some clubs have days related to International Women's Day and they've done something for a few years. They invite women down so they can meet other women and go to the game together and some people said that they've carried on going. I think that's just so lovely.

'Caz was especially delighted that Crawley Town signed a partnership on 25 February 2022. They may not be the highest-profile club to join but it meant that, for the 2022 International Women's Day, there would be a League Two Her Game Too derby between them and her beloved Bristol

Rovers. They had a few women from a refugee charity come along as well. I thought that was just so nice to spread that message that when they go to football, they sit all together so they don't feel alone, so that they can go together and enjoy the game and they have a social event. It was nice to hear that they've got those things already in place. It was having a partnership with us that built it even more and it's becoming recognisable and that's really how we've been contacting the clubs. Even today I've been speaking to clubs and it's not just clubs in the Football League. We've been trying to reach out to a few women's teams as well in the Women's Championship.

'It would be amazing if we could get one of the Super League teams to partner with us because they're at such a good level. They've got some brilliant players that play in the Euros and with the Women's Euros coming to England next summer it is a great opportunity. I'm going to the opening game in Manchester myself, which I'm really excited about. I haven't been to loads of women's games. Obviously, I support a men's team, but I'm making a conscious effort to go and when you do go you really enjoy it. I hope everyone embraces the Euros like we did for the men, and they get some really big crowds. There's nothing stopping the women from doing well. I think they could go far and it'd be great if they're backed as much as the men are.'

Roberto: 'Like you say, it's how much is down to feeling comfortable coming to football matches, feeling included. It might not happen overnight, but the more it can slowly build, the more that our lasses (as we call them here) feel comfortable coming to the ground. Then you will see. Attendances are starting to rise and that's got to be good for the football club and good for everyone.'

Lucy: 'Exactly, yes. I've started to notice during our campaign seeing dads sharing their daughters' love of playing football and how much they enjoy watching them. This is great for them growing up. It's going to make it a better place for them, which is what we want; it's for the next generation to know that a man and a woman can stand next to each other and enjoy the game of football because it's a universal game with universal rules that's for everyone to understand.'

5.

Born Out of Time:
The Ballad of Lily Parr

LILY PARR was one of football's most deadly strikers in a highly gifted team, and the first woman inducted into the Hall of Fame at the National Football Museum. Depressingly, this would only happen in 2002, after being recommended by author Gail Newsham, and it would be another 17 years before her statue was unveiled. The 5ft 10in scorer of almost 1,000 goals spanning a 31-year career had one major weakness. She was born a century too soon. Indeed, she was 16 in 1921 when the FA notoriously banned women's football for half a century.

During the First World War, when men were away fighting, players like Parr were drawing crowds of over 50,000 as part of Dick, Kerr Ladies FC (the name of the Preston munitions factory where most of the women on the team worked). Based in Preston, Parr was a fierce markswoman, but also a shy, diffident member of the team who would often confer praise on her team-mates rather than accept it for herself.

As described by Steve Fleming in the excellent *Radical Football*[2], the marginalisation of women's football started

---

2   Fleming, S., *Radical Football Jürgen Griesbeck and the Story of Football for Good* p.194, (Pitch Publishing. Kindle Edition).

almost as soon as the game was codified. By the end of the 19th century, not only were women still three decades away from equal voting rights but, 'From the outset, there were voices which attempted to undermine women's football and to keep the game exclusively male, with the *Daily Sketch* reporting, "The first few minutes were sufficient to show that football by women … is totally out of the question. A footballer requires speed, judgement, skill, and pluck. Not one of these four qualities was apparent on Saturday. For the most part, the ladies wandered aimlessly over the field at an ungraceful jog-trot."'

But when it suited them in the war years shorn of a labour force, women's football was actively promoted by male munitions factory managers, who could suddenly see the benefits that football gave women for exercise and morale. Indeed, the FA, faced with the cancellation of all its matches at the end of the 1914/15 season, was in a bind. The national game needed to continue in some form so, they turned to the women now migrating from the family to the factories, especially those creating munitions for the front. This hearty endorsement was a little odd coming after decades of men (and some female doctors) warning that exercise would do irreparable damage to them both physically and psychologically.

Writing a century later in the excellent anthology *Football, She Wrote*[3], Julie Welch was also to receive some startling advice about women and sport: '"They said our fannies would fall out, dear," I was once told by a salty old lady athlete.'

To convince a confused population that the doublespeak of women being unsuitable for football never happened, they needed a strong team and, most importantly, a poster girl. Step forward, Lily Parr.

———

3   Authors, Various, *Football, She Wrote: An Anthology of Women's Writing on the Game* p.17, (Floodlit Dreams. Kindle Edition).

As Welch described her, she was a cross between taller versions of Roy Keane and Billy Bremner. Indeed, shockingly for the prudes at the FA desperate for the men to return from war and restore the patriarchy, Lily and Hilda Durbar of Stoke United were sent off for fighting in April 1921 in front of 13,000 fans, eight short months before the guillotine came down on women's football. For men to be men, women had to be 'women' – not occupying jobs or galloping around in shorts, covered in mud, with dirt under their fingernails and all their hair cut off. Our boys had fought and suffered for four years to preserve our way of life.

Their reward had to be to come home and find that way of life waiting for them. In 1921 all four football associations of Great Britain banned women's football as being 'quite unsuitable for females'.

Remarkably, when the men came home from the war, advice to women about exercise took another U-turn. As Welch went on to describe in her essay, *The Girls of '72*: 'The medical profession was called upon once again to endorse the directive.

One Dr Elizabeth Sloan Chesser said: "They may receive injuries from which they may never recover." Dr Mary Scharlieb of Harley Street added: "I consider it a most unsuitable game, too much for a woman's physical frame." It had to be women who delivered the stab in the back. They were denied the use of pitches, and officials and clubs were warned that disciplinary action would result if they assisted the women's game in any way.[4]

Understandably in the face of these bans, and backchannelling by the FA, the women's game went into decline. But passionate players like Parr carried on regardless. Playing on village greens and anywhere else they could create

---

4 Authors, Various, *Football, She Wrote: An Anthology of Women's Writing on the Game* pp.14-5, (Floodlit Dreams. Kindle Edition).

a pitch, her team even toured America in 1922 to temporarily escape the ban (unfortunately Canada upheld the FA's ban on arrival). The nine games played against America's strongest male teams returned three victories, three draws and three losses. An astonishing achievement.

But Lily was to have the last laugh. On 8 September 1937, 16 years into the ban on women's football, Preston Ladies (the new name for Dick, Kerr Women's FC) beat Edinburgh Ladies 5-1 to secure 'the championship of Great Britain and the World'. Lily scored and would join her victorious team-mates at a World Championship Victory Dinner in the swanky surroundings of Booths Cafe in Preston. The faceless FA misogynists faded to black but, standing proudly at the National Football Museum in Manchester since 2019, a statue of Lily dares football to regress back to those dark days of male privilege and, with left foot coiled to score yet another screamer, proudly proclaims that football is Her Game Too.

Fast forward to early May 2022: outside the Emirates Stadium as Arsenal Women beat Spurs, the first (albeit temporary) statue of a current women's player stood proudly. Adidas had created the all-red Vivianne Miedem homage to celebrate the career of the Barclays FA Women's Super League's all-time top scorer. A footballing icon for the Gunners and Holland on the pitch and a LGBTQ+ one off it, she is also a member of Common Goal and commits one per cent of her wages to community organisations helping young people. By the time you read this, we can only hope that 'temporary' is replaced by 'permanent' ...

NB: I owe a huge debt of gratitude to Gail Newsham for fact-checking some of the stories written about Lily that lacked her ferocious research and extensive connections with the Parr family.

6

In Conversation with Her Game Too Director and Advisor Natalie Atkinson

IN KEEPING with the Bezos Day One philosophy, which I touch on in chapter 15 (where Natalie's other role as director of engagement for Fair Game UK is reviewed) the announcement of Her Game Too's partnership with Everton on 26 December 2021 and the appointment of Natalie as the campaign's director and advisor beautifully illustrated Jeff Bezos's key business philosophy. For him, a sharp focus on being a perpetual start-up keeps any organisation on the front foot. This is exactly where Her Game Too find themselves as this book is sent to print exactly on their first anniversary and is published just after the Women's Euros is completed. In their first year, HGT have evolved from a start-up of two football-mad Bristolians into an SME (Small to medium-sized enterprise). Now is the time to scale up, specialise and call on the knowledge base of people like Natalie to avoid losing momentum when moving into their second year. As I mentioned in my other conversation with Natalie, her experience as former managing director of Oldham Athletic and CEO of Southport FC and now the CEO of FC United of Manchester make her key to writing the next Her Game

Too chapter. As Bezos shared with *Forbes* magazine in April 2017: 'The outside world can push you into Day Two if you won't or can't embrace powerful trends quickly. If you fight them, you're probably fighting the future. Embrace them and you have a tailwind.'

What Bezos fights for in the organisation of 55,000 UK workers is a nimble, innovative and energised approach. He is lucky to be operating in a highly competitive but flexible environment where aspiration drives inspiration. Her Game Too campaign in a football environment that carries a heavy burden of history, slowing down decision making and often mitigating against creative input. Bezos fights this kind of glacial pace of change through what he calls 'high-velocity decision making' and a 'disagree and commit' culture. They require action, accountability and a fair level of corporate bravery. A global footballing organisation is likely to be mired in vested interests and a focus on consensus over innovation. Bezos has a powerful antidote to organisational paralysis: 'Invention is by its very nature disruptive. If you want to be understood at all times, then don't do anything new.'

This theme of women's football as a disruptive force for good was amplified by N3XT's January 2022 report: Enabling Women's Football to Disrupt the Industry. The extensive and upbeat report was overseen by eight highly respected voices including Polly Bancroft (general manager at Brighton and Hove Albion), Bianca Rech (sporting director women's football at FC Bayern Munich) and Courtney Ksiazek (the senior director, partnership marketing at the intriguing new club Angel City FC). The executive summary authored by director of women's football at N3XT Sports, Arianna Criscione, is brimming with positivity and determination that women's football will not provide more of what the men's offering but will, 'become the fastest and most disruptive force in the football and sporting industry in the decade to come'. It points out something else that chimes with Bezos's approach: how the women's game has a chance to collegially shape the future with a vibrancy that is not weighed down by the bureaucracy clogging up the oversight of the men's game.

'We find ourselves with a whiteboard in front of us where we can craft a shared vision for the future of the women's game that disrupts the status quo of the beautiful game,' writes Cricione. 'The window of opportunity is here, and yet it grows narrower by the day. If we do not take bold and imminent action to propel the women's game, it will remain dependent on, and fall victim to, the structure of the men's game.'

***

I see a lot of this in Caz and Lucy. I had no intention of writing this book but, after seeing them at Exeter City's St James Park Stadium the day before my birthday in August 2021, I was blown away by their dynamic, front-foot approach to tackling the dark forces of misogyny that many other women have despaired over. For these two, compliance was acceptance: confrontation was the only option. And all this while watching their beloved Bristol Rovers get battered 4-1 by Exeter City. Bezos's philosophy is all about a focus on results and not process. His 'disagree and commit' system understands that universal agreement is rare but that it's still possible for people who disagree to work towards the same goal. He believes that his tide of progress can carry those that don't buy into it but accept its inevitability and offers global gains for the greater good. This also fits perfectly with the HGT philosophy that finds ways over, around and under obstacles to reach targets by using intelligent pressure applied relentlessly.

But football has something that Bezos will never create. Clubs are bursting with shared values and emotional connections spanning generations. This is why the evolving organisation that Her Game Too has become needs Natalie's perspective, passion and experience to turn the huge range of incredible projects into a coherent, mature and effective process that never forgets its their vital and unstoppable Day One philosophy.

***

I caught up with Natalie in January 2022 to find out more about her new role.

Matt: 'Please tell us about your football career so far.'

Natalie: 'I have always been a football fan; my team is Manchester City. I started as CEO at Curzon Ashton which was one of the best roles I have had – from developing the community, establishing a community foundation, increasing the fan base, working with the incredible volunteers, the FA Cup run we had and working with a board of directors that gave everything to their club – I will always have fond memories. I then moved to a huge project professionally with Southport FC, I stayed for 12 months to manage with the new owner a stadium rebuild, build an off-field team, establish a community foundation, increase the fan base, and redevelop the stadia pitch. I then moved to Oldham Athletic as MD – a challenging role, a passionate fan base that wants to see success back at Boundary Park. I steadied the club off the field for 18 months and I am proud that the workforce and team that I managed delivered the vision we had off the field. I had a team of over 150 from the academy to the business team – we set targets and achieved them. This only works when you have buy-in from the owner! I have, in the last 12 months, graduated from UCFB/VSI completing my CEO of a Sports Organisation course and become the director of engagement of Fair Game.'

Matt: 'What was it about Her Game Too that inspired you to become their director and advisor?' Natalie: 'Having been involved in football for several years I have seen and been subjected to the nasty side of the game mainly via social media, but some instances face to face. The campaign is inspirational and I can see that through hard work, direction and having a strategy in place, HGT will have a huge impact on fans, the game and what football looks like off the field in leadership roles in clubs. I am really passionate about change and in particular how we educate fans that no form of abuse will be tolerated within the game. My job is to advise and guide the HGT team by linking to stakeholders, ensuring that our message is clear and helping them write a strategy for the future.'

Matt: 'What are the personal and professional qualities you feel you add to the campaign?'

Natalie: 'Determination to succeed and wanting change. I want the campaign to leave a legacy wherever it goes or wherever it may take us. Focus, organisation, and transparency are key qualities that I will also bring.'

Matt: 'What are the key targets for the campaign in 2022 and beyond?'

Natalie: 'We would like to see a campaign that isn't a one-day event but a campaign that is embraced every day. Our core objectives both short term and more long term include: an education programme delivered in schools working with club foundations; 92 partner clubs; being established as a community interest company; a major sponsor and a paid workforce.'

Matt: 'When Everton partnered with your campaign, how do you think that changed people's perceptions of Her Game Too?'

Natalie: 'It was a game-changer – having a Premier League club as part of the campaign is huge. The whole club are backing the campaign – men's and women's teams – this shows how far the campaign has come. Everton are the first of many. We would like every PL club to be part of the campaign. Everton are the people's club and for them to stand out and be the first is testament to the club.'

Matt: 'There are a growing number of campaigns that support inclusivity in football. What are the unique selling points of Her Game Too?'

Natalie: 'It was established by fans with real stories. The team have real-time jobs and careers, they are doing this in their spare time, they have been subjected to terrible abuse and have had the courage to stand up for what they believe in.'

Matt: 'How do you feel about the progress being made to make football more welcoming to women during your time in football?'

Natalie: 'I think it's slow, and that's why I wanted to get involved in the campaign. If we do not start to speak out, challenge and push some boundaries the game won't change – not on the field as we are moving in the right direction [but] I believe off the field progress is very slow. We know that the number of women working in clubs is getting less – I have research within the EFL/National League that indicates that the number of females in management roles is two per cent. It needs to change!

Matt: 'We are talking before the Women's Euros and this book will be published after the tournament ends. What are your predictions for England?'

Natalie: 'I firmly believe the team can win the Euros!'

7.

Breaching the Grass Ceiling.
The Power of Pathfinders

'It feels like women's football is not
really having a moment, but it's having
a movement.'[5]

Andrea Ekblad, rights director DAZN

IN JANUARY 2022, to help build profile and momentum for the UEFA Women's Euros, £500,000 was awarded by the National Lottery to a project telling the story of England's pathfinding football women. A database was created, starting in 1972 (the first year after the half-century ban), of every England player, captain, goalscorer and match score, running parallel with the information already available in the men's game. Two key points really stand out for me. Firstly, that this information will be shared through the FA's England Football website, and secondly, that there will be a focus on the LGBTQ+ community in women's football. As I found out, the stories are inspirational and compelling.

---

5   *Alex Scott: The Future of Women's Football*, BBC June 2022

Sharing the Passion. Helen Nkwocha

After reading her recent interview with Sky Sports, I was intrigued to find out more about what drives this former south London policewoman to keep pushing boundaries in the game. She's now based in Iceland and when I spoke to her, Helen Nkwocha was settling into her stint as head coach of Betri Deildin League team Tvoroyrar Boltfelag in the Faroe Islands. It wasn't only the league and location that piqued media interest, but also the fact that Helen was the first woman to coach a top-flight men's team in Europe. Talking to Helen in her office in late October 2021, just before training as her team prepared to face B68 Toftir, it was still dark outside. Helen knew she had a hectic day ahead as, after training, it would be her that needed to put together the tactical analysis video ahead of Sunday's match as well as all the administration that comes with the role. But what struck me was that, among the tactic boards and other paraphernalia of a hectic football sanctuary in the background of our Zoom call, here was a coach – not a woman or man, but a coach – at peace with her role and life decisions. Money was tight, success on the field was elusive, but job satisfaction was complete.

Matt: 'What I'd really like to do is get a sense of your drive and passion. I read the Sky Sports headline of you as the first female coach of a top-flight men's team, but for me, it's about that journey you've been on, the choices that you've made.'

Helen: 'I didn't realise it was such a big thing. I just decided: this is what I want because I don't think I've ever been different. I joined the police and at 20, after four-and-a-half years, I was acting sergeant. It just didn't seem unusual to me. I saw it as normal: everyone in my family is quite similar, to be honest with you. So, the way I am with my coaching career is that it seems quite natural.'

Matt: 'What amazed me was how you essentially were on a treadmill of a career path and a house owner. For most people that is that: you are locked in and the process will continue until you retire. Did people think that was a bit unusual, that you just chose to jump off the treadmill like that?'

Helen: 'Yes. I think everybody was like, "Helen: what are you doing?" Because you're over a certain age and all your friends around you are doing what they should be doing for that age. They go on holiday once or twice a year and they're working hard and they're settled. You're doing what you should do for being in your mid-30s.

'There wasn't a reason for me to stay doing something that I wasn't passionate about anymore.'

Matt: 'Was there a moment when you realised it was time to change or was it a process where you felt you were losing your passion for your job but wanted to pursue your true passion of coaching?'

Helen: 'It was a process. A lot of people at the time in the police would have business interests, so you might be someone who's got a shop or you have someone who is a referee. A couple of us were also coaches. On my days off, I was still playing. I was playing at a decent level as well and then suddenly I wasn't anymore. I started to get into my coaching and realised that I was really enjoying it. It was a big challenge and I loved it. It was very, very hard though. I started to think of other things that I could do to allow myself to still do coaching and so I started thinking of different ideas like getting a coffee shop. I enjoy law so I thought maybe I should look into becoming a solicitor. In the end, I just thought, well, how about you coach more and see whether or not it's something that you can really do.

'So, I started to work night shifts for one year and that allowed me to coach during the daytime. But I was actually becoming sick. I was literally grey. because I was having two hours of sleep or so for the planning and delivery of sessions. It's not just that you show up at training. You spend a couple of hours planning and then it turned out that I was really enjoying it, but I wasn't fit for purpose. I wasn't able to do my police work properly because I was so tired all the time. I wasn't functioning very well and I decided that I didn't want to do this anymore.'

Matt: 'What intrigues me is that you needed to get out of bed for work because you had bills to pay, but you didn't have to be depriving yourself of sleep to do the coaching. What was it that made you think, "I've only had two hours of sleep but I have to do the coaching"?'

Helen: 'I never thought twice. Looking back now, I don't remember ever thinking, "Oh I don't really want to do this." I always remember feeling quite buoyant about it. So, I think that feeling was what kept me going because I never stopped wanting to do it.'

Matt: 'Maybe you felt, even subconsciously, that you had found your vocation?'

Helen: 'It started to feel like that.'

Matt: 'You said in one of your interviews that you don't see yourself as a trailblazer. *The Guardian* did a nice interview with Hope Powell yesterday. I know you describe her as a real role model for you. What is it that you feel about her, that inspires you more than anything?'

Helen: 'Well, one of the comments on the Sky Sports Twitter account (and actually, they were all quite negative comments about me doing this job), was that I only got the interview because of my colour and it couldn't possibly be because of my potential. Well, if that's the case, wouldn't I have got every interview that I have applied for?

'I didn't have what Hope Powell had and I've heard so many stories where people have been judging her just because she existed and she dared to do this job and she dared to do this coaching course. Coaching is such a small world, especially if you're from London. You tend to know each other. You meet them on courses. You see them in the clubs and you have discussions. Or you overhear discussions. And I'd heard so many negative things about her and it made me realise that's what she has to go through.'

Matt: 'I wanted to ask about your time so far in the Faroe Islands. It's a fascinating place that should be the set for the *Game of Thrones*, but in terms of your day-to-day coaching, what's it been like so far?'

Helen: 'I think there's a lot of transitions happening because we have a couple of teams here that are very successful. [The league leaders when we spoke, Klaksvíkar Ítróttarfelag, had either won the title or been runners-up 32 times, whilst current champions Havnar Bóltfelag had been champions or runners-up an astonishing 49 times. For context, Helen's team had won seven titles and been runners-up ten times. Klaksvíkar Ítróttarfelag would go on to stroll to the title by nine points after their final game on 30 October 2021.] The top teams qualify regularly for the European competitions so that allows them to have more staff. It allows them to have much broader facilities and attract different types of people to the club, especially money to buy more players of a higher quality. They get to play in the Champions League and Europa Conference and so I think the rest of the clubs are starting to realise, there's a big difference between us and them.

Matt: 'That's a shame to hear, but I also work for an organisation called Fair Game UK which tries to look at financial fairness. And you know that so many clubs in the UK are financial basket cases, particularly in the Championship. Do you still feel it's a relatively level playing field in your league?'

Helen: 'There's not necessarily a difference in playing ability, it's the level of investment and education. Right now, our players are quite low in confidence, so they might be more inclined to abandon tactics you've planned in the week during practice and there is the added challenge of the extra scrutiny because I'm female. That's why there's been more attention. But you know, we've been involved in football for ages, and we know that teams get relegated and promoted.

You can't do everything. I'm not a magician, but in terms of the development of the players, that has been my high focus.

'So, whoever comes in and works with these players, do they understand this part of a training session and how it appeared in the game? Are we connecting how we operate during the week with how we operate at the weekend? Do we appear to be a modern team or club? Do we show clear principles to show clear game understanding: that's been what I've used in my mind as a key target when I talk to players, when I communicate with them and when we train.'

Matt: 'I'm really interested in your Immersed in the Game website, where you focus a lot on visual imagery. What is it about images that you find effective or a good way to get an idea across that may be different to a lot of words or tactics on a page or a whiteboard?

Helen: 'Football players have the best ability to problem-solve of any other sports person. So, the game is visual and the problem-solving is instantaneous. We need to recognise that the skill set is already there, that they can solve visual problems. Something I acquired from Hope Powell was watching her managing one of the national team games. There was a break in play and she got all the players in and everyone was around the tactics board. They had about two minutes and everyone got in and got their instructions. That's a different way to communicate, but that's for us as coaches to be creative and try and find the ways to hit the visual in the players as quickly as possible and see if it's effective. Some players prefer you to talk to them or at them.'

Matt: 'From your point of view, as an experienced and well-travelled coach, what is it that you hope for the future of how the football world will look?'

Helen: 'You just want freedom of movement. What do you do for a job? I'm a football player. OK, great. And you want people who are key decision-makers to recognise that co-ed training is effective. That's part of the education of coaches and it's part of players' understanding. Have we explained to them the benefits? Do we encourage them? I think in the future I'd like to see clubs encouraging female players up until the age of 14 to recognise that there is no big difference in playing in a way that allows you to still enjoy the game. I love listening to Karen Carney and we're of the same playing era. You just listen to her and if I'm just listening to somebody who has got excellent insight on the game; it doesn't have to be a male or a female voice.'

Born To Do It: Fleur Robinson

In an interview with the *Daily Telegraph*'s chief sports reporter Jeremy Wilson, on 26 October 2021, Fleur Robinson described a life immersed in the fabric of football. Wilson wrote: 'She also has hands-on, grassroots experience of football basics including contracts, ticketing, health and safety, hospitality and operating a turnstile. It's fair to say Fleur has experienced it all during her 24 years working at the club.'

Robinson has also spoken to Women in Football about her career: 'In fact, the only job I haven't done is cut the grass on the club tractor!'

After a career plotting the rise of League One club Burton Albion, Fleur dropped to the National League for an intriguing challenge with Wrexham where she became chief executive in March 2021. The headline writers were buzzing around the story of Hollywood actors Ryan Reynolds and Rob McElhenney being the new owners, but Robinson's story is just as compelling.

Wilson went on to describe how, 'The first black female CEO of a professional football club, Robinson was this week named on football's prestigious Black List for influential role models within the national game. It is the second time she has appeared on the list and, while she says that "people don't particularly see me as being a woman of colour", some of the experiences of her father remain etched in her mind.'

Like Helen Nkwocha, Robinson doesn't see herself as a role model, preferring to be part of a sustainable and forward-looking movement for a more inclusive game. 'It needs people to talk about the roles in sport. You do see things changing slowly.'

The glacial speed of change is slowly starting to thaw at the Football Association, where Robinson was appointed to the Council in 2016. Finally, slowly, there appear to be moves being made towards shaping an organisation more representative of the communities it serves. But Robinson is realistic, telling reporter Wilson: 'There are challenges. I see it now. You go to a boardroom and people gravitate to the male party you are with as opposed to you as a female. That's the generation change that needs to happen. Any organisation needs to have that diverse workforce to bring different cultures together to create ideas. And it's not just the boardroom. I'm also a big advocate for the administration support within football.'

For Fleur, challenges are opportunities for progress. As she shared with Women in Football: 'Football has changed a lot over the years and there are many more females involved in the game, and also in key roles. But like most industries, there are not as many as there should be and certainly not at a senior level.

'At the end of the day in every walk of life, we all have a responsibility to open up opportunities for all. In football, this means looking at policies and promoting more opportunities for women within football, which has certainly come a long way.

'I'm really looking forward to playing a part in the development of women in football and can see exciting opportunities ahead.'

Hope Springs Eternal

In the week I spoke to Helen, Hope Powell gave a major interview to *The Guardian* that showed just why she is a pathfinder for her fellow Londoners.[6] A playing career collecting 66 England caps transitioned, unusually, into being a national coach first with England (the first time the post had been full time) and then Great Britain's Olympic squad before moving to club coaching with Brighton and Hove Albion in 2017 (a post she still held at the time of writing). Hope's playing career took off at 16 when she won her first England cap as an attacking midfielder who would go on to score 35 international goals. As England coach, she oversaw root-and-branch changes from battling against the all-male hierarchy of the FA to lay down pathways from under-15 teams, to coach mentoring and use of the National Player Development Centre at Loughborough University.

By 2009 she was in a position to offer central player contracts to encourage full-time training and had also found time to be the first woman to receive coaching's highest qualification: the UEFA Pro Licence.

Talking to reporter Tumaini Carayol, Powell's story arc describes being rejected by her school team because of her gender to becoming England manager at 31. She racked up a brace of firsts as the premier black and female England women's coach. Powell is in the perfect position to assess the rise of women's football.

---

6   Carayol, T. 'How Hope Powell became a football legend: "I'm not afraid of anybody."' *The Guardian*, 21 October 2021, https://www.theguardian. com/football/2021/oct/21/how-hope-powell-became-a-football-legend-im-not-afraid-of-anybody. Accessed 24 October 2021.

'Back then, everything about women's football was different. It is night and day,' she says. 'Now, you treat it as a job, whereas before you had to train on your own, you had to work or go to school and then fit the training in. We used to train on concrete surfaces in schools ... We paid subs back then to play. We had to buy our own boots, wash our own kit ... It's a different world.'

This was richly illustrated on 25 October 2021, when Powell unveiled a purpose-built £8.5m women's training facility for her Brighton players, that mirrored the men's. It is not only a strident statement by the club about breaking into the WSL European places, but another step further away from Hope's past of training on car park concrete and towards enabling an excellence-focussed environment for all girls and women pursuing a footballing career.

Talking to the *Daily Mail*, Powell eloquently identified one of the key engines for change embraced by Brighton to evolve the women's game: 'We want to make sure that everything is really integrated and capture what it means to be at Brighton. Having a presence on the main board gives us that connectivity so that we know the women's game is integral to all our conversations.' [7]

Hope is acutely aware of her role and responsibility as a pathfinder and her persistence was key.

'I was prepared to ask questions and quite often accept the fact that some things would be a "no" and just choose my moments to ask again,' she says. 'It was all about trying to make everything better for players, the staff, so that we could move the game forward, because, after all, I was managing a team and we wanted to win.'

Hope, like Helen, has a positive mindset about the trajectory of the women's game: 'Over the last ten years,

---

7   Batte, K. *Mail Online*, https://www.dailymail.co.uk/sport/womens-football/article-10130173/Brighton-huge-leap-forward-womens-football-unveiling-fantastic-new-training-ground.html

massive strides have been made in the women's game,' she says Powell. 'I think we need to continue to professionalise and make sure there is parity across the board.'

In her 2016 autobiography *Hope: My Life in Football* she said she was acutely aware of being born half a decade before the FA's medieval half-century ban on women's football was lifted. She also has a keen sense of the history that laid foundations for her career. The rising interest in women's football during the Second World War is well documented, but it was also strengthened with capable coaching by invalided men returning from the front. As she describes, 'Women's football developed from being a novelty to serious sporting business.'

Powell's personality warmed to these trailblazing women who were to raise huge sums for the war effort through their football skills, which chimed with her own values of determined defiance:

'If I was going to get on in life – and get the life I wanted – I knew I would have to fight and scrap for it.'

This need to fight was brought into sharp relief when, despite playing for England, Powell was banned from playing for her school team purely because she was female. But enlightened support for Powell's developing career would come from a surprising source. Millwall became the first club in the country to open a Girls' Centre of Excellence in 1971 (the year that the FA lifted its odious ban) where they would, 'help develop young footballers from the age of eight right up to senior level'. Despite, or because of, Millwall men's poor reputation, this project was a chance for the club to show a more inclusive and enlightened approach and did hundreds of female footballers the power of good.

Talking at the 2015 Soccer Development Conference, Powell eloquently described her furious work ethic in her quest to create meaningful traction for the women's game: 'I think putting players on central contracts in England was a huge boost for the game. The players were having to combine their everyday working lives with training and football, which are huge demands. I think any player knows if you want to be at the top of your game, you're talking about having to be almost a full-time athlete, training every day.

'It was hard work. I had to put a budget together to explain why it would be a good thing and then we were able to get, at that time, 20 players on full-time FA contracts that, combined with their club contracts, meant that they could dedicate themselves to training and football without having the added pressures of work.

'I think my personality allowed me to do that as much as anything. I had a really good playing career. I was an international player very young. I had an extensive career that spanned some 15 or 16 years as an international so I was quite credible. The main challenges were to convince the Football Association that investing in the women's game was a good thing to do and if we invested in it the chances are that we will be successful.'

In June 2022, Powell's Merit award, given by the PFA for her outstanding contribution to the women's game, showed just how universally she was respected. Her response to the award was typically endearing and honest.

'I have never been afraid to ask questions and challenge people. I think I have helped shape the game and drive it forward along with lots of other people. I'm hoping I'll be remembered as someone who was passionate and wanted the best for women's football on a local and national level.'

Mariela Nisotaki

It's not just that Mariela was made head of emerging talent for intermittent Premier League club Norwich City in September 2021 that serves as an inspiration to other women in football, but that she has developed a career path at the club for almost half a decade, showing dedication, progression and stability. After arriving at Carrow Road as a first-team technical scout in January 2017, she spent almost two years developing skills and networks around the club and through the league before making the step up to become lead recruitment analyst. After a year in that role, Mariela was made European and domestic league scout in June 2019. After another one-year stint as lead technical and intelligence scout, she made her latest transition to become the head of emerging talent. Now firmly established as part of the club's coaching hierarchy, she has not only highlighted a position but a pathway for the right candidate, regardless of gender, to follow.

Talking to Training Ground Guru's reporter Simon Austin in October 2021, Nisotaki said that in all the scouting she had done for the club across Europe, only Eintracht Frankfurt and Espanyol also employed female scouts, with Helena Costa in Germany and Andrea Orts in Spain.

Costa joined the scouting team in 2017 after coaching experience at Celtic and head coach roles with the Qatar and Iran women's teams. Three years before joining Frankfurt she made the notable breakthrough of being the first woman to manage a men's team in the two top divisions of a major European league when she took charge of Clermont Foot 63. He was signed the same year as Costa and was the only female scout in La Liga. But the pleasing news was that the club sought her extensive knowledge of South American football rather than her gender. Indeed, Orts has had more pushback about her age than her sex, which shows a refreshing outlook by the club to hire based on addressing a need rather than pursuing a vacuous publicity stunt.

Not only does Nisotaki embrace being a pathfinder, but she is also scoping out a newly created club position focussing on talent identification of players in their late teens and early twenties both in the UK and across the globe. She adopts a positive mindset about her situation, considering her position as a woman in a male-dominated industry as an opportunity rather than a threat. Talking to *Eastern Daily*

Press journalist Connor Southwell in October 2021, she commented: 'One thing I always say is that your difference is probably your strength, whether it's women in football or something else.'

She added: 'So, for me, it's an advantage. If you are working hard enough and you are confident in yourself, it's an advantage because people remember me. If I go to a stadium they remember, "this is Mariela from Norwich", so that's good. It's challenging but that's good. It's challenging for everyone when you are working in professional football – for women and men.'

Mariela shows the true traits of a pathfinder: indefatigable drive, tenacity and resilience. As Matthew Syed describes in his definitive book on the winning mindset, *Black Box Thinking*, people at the vanguard of change need to adopt a constructive approach to pushbacks: '... the explanation for success hinges, in powerful and often counter-intuitive ways, on how we react to failure.'[8]

But, rather than the binary status of preventing failure and aiming for success, Mariela has started to create a culture not only through her professionalism but by the way her club have handed her long-term responsibility, inviting her to step up and take ownership of her career. They have energised her environment with a sense of purpose and, in return, she has used the environment of mutual support and enfranchisement to richly repay her employers and eloquently illustrate the value of diverse thought.

***

Slowly, surely, people like Helen, Hope Mariela and Fleur are building a momentum that has profound implications for the growth of women's football. With deep roots, building

---

8   Syed, M., *Black Box Thinking: The Surprising Truth About Success* p.8, (John Murray Press. Kindle Edition).

momentum and an increasing global consensus, these four women and many like them are creating a fairer, more diverse and better future for everyone in the game.

8.

Innovation. Exeter City's Her Game Too Weekend

TALKING TO journalist Cameron Cairns for a podcast @ CameronCairns87, on 26 October 2021, co-founder Amy Clement showed the overwhelming excitement that being part of HGT creates. When asked about her favourite parts of being involved in the movement, she said: 'One will definitely have to be releasing the shirt. That is so exciting, and I can't wait for people to get them. I can't wait to develop that side of things as well. Every meeting I have, I enjoy. Every meeting opens up another door, another partnership, an idea, an event. There is not a boring day, ever, which is really good.'

Amy continued, 'If we announce something, or if we get tagged in things, we see kids in their Her Game Too tops. Everything like that is just incredible, as it just shows how far the message has gone. It shows how far Her Game Too has reached already and we're only five months old now. I'm really pleased with how it's all going, and it's just fantastic … This shows that the ceiling for Her Game Too is so high, that the sky really is the limit for this fantastic set of female supporters … They should all be so proud!'

The group zings with new ideas and clubs respond in kind. One superb example of energising support came from HGT partner club Rochdale on 7 March 2022, when free tickets were on offer for every female secondary school pupil in the Rochdale Borough for any match in March to celebrate their Her Game Too connections. For Tiverton Town, it was only £1 for local girls and women's players for their game celebrating 2022's International Women's Day. Bournemouth came up with innovative support for their women's team on International Women's Day 2022. The players warmed up for their game against Peterborough in shirts with the Bournemouth women's team's names on the back and used the front to promote their fixture against Chesham United, while Bristol Rovers scored a UK first on 23 April 2022. The men's team were at home to Forest Green Rovers and the women started their game immediately afterwards, in the same stadium. This could make the groundsman blow a gasket, but it created a wonderful opportunity to truly act as one club.

***

This leads us beautifully to the Her Game Too/Exeter City Weekend …

For the Trust-owned League Two club Exeter City the first Her Game Too connection came on Saturday, 21 August 2021. They were playing Bristol Rovers and the game was dedicated to the campaign. with Caz and Lucy (two diehard Gasheads) were special guests. The event was remarkable not only for the rotating pitchside electronic HGT logos and posters around the ground supporting their cause, but because City were 4-0 up after 24 minutes! Caz and Lucy probably wanted to be anywhere else but the pitch at half-time introducing themselves to the ecstatic City fans, but they handled it with their usual good grace.

Exeter are not alone in using match days to celebrate their support of Her Game Too but, on the weekend of 16 and 17 October 2021, they took that connection an innovative step further than any other club had at the time. With the men's team playing at St James Park on the Saturday against Newport County and the women's team on the following day in a Devon Cup match against local rivals Plymouth Argyle (their first match at St James Park since 2019), 48 hours were bundled together as a Her Game Too Weekend.

In the week leading up to the games, the club's social media team of Craig, Scott and Jed promoted the weekend as a bespoke festival of football, as well as highlighting some of the appalling abuse some female fans have to endure by sharing the quotes from Caz and Lucy's recent survey of female fans that you'll read in the appendix. Videos were also made to increase the women players' profiles, featuring first-teamers Mia Preston and Manfy Sharpe, while the heartbreaking but inspiring story of Shiva Shoaee, an Iranian woman who moved to Exeter in 2021 served as a moving tribute to the club. She said: 'When it comes to equality in football, the first thing that pops into your mind is the wages that women players get and they are complaining to have equal pay. However, in other parts of the world, in the Middle East, Iranian women have been fighting for their right to go into stadiums and watch football for almost 40 years. For some 40 years, women have been largely banned from attending soccer matches at Iran's stadiums. But under pressure from FIFA, soccer's governing body, Iranian authorities are allowing a few thousand women to watch a game in 2021 at Tehran's Azadi Stadium – in a section separate from men.'

Shiva continued, on the video: 'Last January I came to the UK, and when I settled in Exeter, I started to do some research about its football team and found that Exeter football history went back to 1904! What a team!

'Finally, the gates are open for me. The first match I came to at the "home of football" was one of the sweetest memories I have ever had! Exeter 4 Bristol Rovers 1. I still can't believe it's happening because, after all these years of watching every match on TV, I'm able to experience everything in person. I'll be able to feel the stands and closely watch the game. That's absolutely fabulous.'

Shiva's story was picked up by BBC Sport on 7 March 2022. Talking to their reporter Brent Pilnick, she related how her time watching the Grecians helped her cope with her mother's death in the summer of 2021 and being unable to travel for her funeral due to the pandemic.

'This was something that really changed my life during these few months, just to be in the atmosphere and be among those lovely people that are supporting their team,' she explained.

'This is something I feel is really changing my life. I don't need any therapy or grief consultant, that's the power of football and it's something really unique that I had experienced in my life.'

Finally, she shared with Pilnick her hope for the future: 'My dream is to have a chance to go to a stadium one day in Iran with all my friends, my family, my cousins and sit beside my brothers and share my passion with them,' she said.

A truly inspirational figure supporting a club I am proud to be a (small-part) owner of.

***

The men's team warmed up before Saturday's game wearing Her Game Too shirts while the women's team were in and around the stadium engaging with fans and the VIP suite was decked out in HGT logos. Caz was the guest of honour and, after being led to her dining room seat, was overwhelmed to see the club's efforts: placing an HGT T-shirt on her table along with a personalised letter welcoming her and even a free pint for her and her boyfriend Ollie.

For the Sunday game, VIP tickets were made available including silver service meals. The City boardroom was repurposed so that fans and sponsors of the women's team could meet and greet members of the club and share ideas about how to plot the future.

The idea of refocussing the boardroom to drive the women's game forward was taken to another level on 31 May, 2022, when Cambridge United launched a new Women's Football Board that would integrate and drive forward the women's team in the club. Chair of the board Jenny Horsfield told Cambridge United's media team:

'Women's and girls' football has a huge impact in the community and we very much want to ensure that Cambridge United is at the forefront of innovation and inspiration to local girls and women who love the game.'

The new Women's Football Board fed directly into the Cambridge United Board after their first meeting on 6 June.

***

Like many teams in the FA Women's National League (England's third tier) Exeter City Women play 'away' every week. For the women Grecians, a 'home' game happens 20km away in sleepy Cullompton, so chances to connect and network with a mass of local fans and sponsors in Exeter itself are rare. They still achieve some of the league's highest attendances, which speaks volumes for the dedication of their fans. As a season ticket holder, I am put to shame by their determination to be there week in and week out.

Local girls and women's teams were contacted and asked to support the game en masse, and for every adult coming to the Sunday game, a child could accompany them for free. After both matches, Her Game Too warm-up T-shirts were then signed and auctioned off for charity.

Caz was understandably delighted when asked by the Exeter City media team for her response to the Her Game Too weekend. 'We are so excited to see the first professional football fixture weekend dedicated to #HerGameToo and for it to commence so quickly after we launched,' she said.

'Exeter City, Newport County and Plymouth Argyle have been brilliant in supporting the campaign, so it is fitting they play each other for these dedicated fixtures.

'We would like to thank Exeter City for this fantastic gesture and I'm sure their female supporters are exceptionally proud of their club for all their support surrounding #HerGameToo so far.'

The campaign was also fully backed by the players. City favourite Pierce Sweeney spoke for so many fathers when he said, 'If my daughter grows up and ever wants to play football, I don't understand why that should be an issue to anyone.'

Supporting Sweeney, talking to *When Saturday Comes* journalist Catherine Etoe for February 2022's edition, club media officer Craig Bratt added: 'Often the things said to female supporters are passed off as banter, and the point we wanted to make is, it actually isn't banter. We want to make female supporters confident enough to react to something being said to them rather than just leaving it be.'

This was a view backed up by co-founder of HGT Eve Ralph in conversation with Jobs4Football's Liam Kennedy in February 2022. 'The word banter gets thrown around quite a bit and it's time to understand that these comments aren't banter.'

***

The day would be a carnival of joy and comradeship but while walking from the St James Park train station to the ground, my wife and I heard why Her Game Too matters. Two men were separately going to the stadium with their daughters who were all dressed in Exeter's red and white. Noticing that both men were going to the same event, one acknowledged the other by saying, 'Are you going to the game?' The other replied, in front of both girls, 'Yeah, but it's not really a game, is it? It's only a women's game.' So dispiriting.

But that couldn't dampen the historical day. Not only did the phenomenal work of supporters and other local groups' drive the record attendance of 1,372 (beating Chelsea women's crowd against Wolfsburg in the Champions League by nine) and build huge awareness of Exeter's women's team, but they enjoyed an impressive media spotlight. ITV's reporter Sam Mangat was suitably impressed when reporting on the double header. Club director Sue McQueenie told him: 'As a supporter-owned club, we need to be doing these kinds of things. Inclusivity is so important and to be raising awareness of these kinds of issues. Luckily, we don't have that many [of] those kinds of things [abusive behaviour towards women] happening here, but I just think it's a really great thing to be doing.'

Devon Live described the day as the 'perfect advert for women's football' and Adam Knee, a staunch City fan, with two football-mad daughters, tweeted: 'I'm not sure any of us will forget today. Well done @ExeterCityWFC you were all fantastic!'

Talking to the club before the match, the Knee family pinpointed how the building power of the women's game is beginning to be harnessed. When asked why they would be at the game, Vikki Knee explained: 'I think mainly down to the media taking quite a lot of interest in women's football generally. But it's just that empowerment of being a female and seeing female players. I think the Women's World Cup was a big thing in our house that really set it off to begin with.'

And the game? Oh, what a glorious game it was. On a day of two Zoes: Plymouth captain Cunningham sent the Pilgrims into a first-half lead with a stunning free kick from distance that went in off the bar, but the Grecians equalised through their own Zoe Watkins in the second half. Despite chances for both sides, the match finished all square and it was the turn of City keeper Abbi Bond to grab the spotlight in a penalty shoot-out, he saved Plymouth's first kick from Tash

Knapman, and one from the Argyle goalscorer in normal time, and City had done it.

The game was the centrepiece of a glorious celebration of women's football progress, a platform for sharing the passion of a committed support base had its day in the Devon sunshine.

***

Marie epitomised the absolute best of us. Joining me in the City boardroom an hour before kick-off, she walked in alone and was uncertain if she should be there as she wasn't a player sponsor (as we are). Softly spoken but clearly a knowledgeable fan, as the football drama unfolded before us, she grew in confidence and joined us for the riotous post-match celebrations in the club bar. A couple of hours after I first met her, she diffidently shared why she had been invited. Proudly removing a singlet from her bag with the City crest on, she explained how she had run a marathon to raise funds for the women's team. The room was electric with inspiring stories of sacrifice, dedication and community that merged into a glorious narrative tapestry as the ciders flowed relentlessly.

The club slogan of One Grecian Goal seemed tailor-made for these 48 hours of football celebrations. The men stumbled to a frustrating 2-2 draw but the women won against a team from the league above in a glorious, high-quality match full of tempo and jeopardy. Hopefully, the two dads revisited their opinions after this technical, tactical and intense encounter played in a rambunctious atmosphere. This was the definition of a proper game, irrespective of gender, orientation or age.

But then, just when the memory of a glorious sunny afternoon began to fade, Exeter's media man Craig Bratt and Sue McQueenie were awarded the Her Game Too Hero Award for October 2021 and the gloriously cider-infused memories just came flooding back …

And just when I thought I couldn't love my local club more, they decided to embed the women's team into the official club website. Using the same format and font as the men's pages, they showed how the women were one more important part of the club.

But it is not just high-profile gestures that help the journey to equality. Club merchandise like birthday cards sent to fans' families have images of City players, male and female, together in size and profile. The match-day programme for the game against Scunthorpe on 16 January 2022 featured City women's captain Manfy Sharpe alongside the men's leader Matt Jay, and posters of the women's team were being sold in the club shop. City went one step further for the game against Hartlepool on 29 January 2022, with the front cover featuring City women's Connie Pengelly in an interview with her about her career as part of a preview of their FA Cup tie with West Brom. Banner events are high in impact, but everyday gestures like this help build the foundations for meaningful change. The Grecians have welcomed the women's game into the fold and showed other clubs how to be a platform for respect, integrity and inclusivity.

Caz and Lucy's beloved Bristol Rovers would take this enlightened approach a step further on 23 April 2022 when, for the game against Forest Green, The Gas men and women played on the same day and on the same pitch. Fans only needed to buy one ticket and to stay to enjoy the women's match. This has become a friendly war of mutual construction. Over to you, City …

9.

The Power of Education

'THERE IS definitely a lot of naivety surrounding the subject and education will play a big part in changing the attitudes and stopping casual sexism.'

On 2021's last day, the Her Game Too Twitter account highlighted a key driver for a future free from misogyny. The beauty of a focus on education is that it allows us to reverse-engineer sexist attitudes and reset flexible minds to reject values that alienate and belittle women. One of the respondents to the Her Game Too Survey neatly identified the key role school plays in forming learned behaviours.

'I believe the mindset was set in schools, as at my school I was told by teachers that football was a boys' game and I'd much prefer to dance.'

It also helps to isolate those who refuse to change or listen, reminiscent of the 'I'm not a racist but' booing on taking the knee before matches that has, thankfully, largely dissipated. By exposing the limits of their logic, we can address it and, as we hear at grounds now, move towards a place of understanding and support. Founder Caz May has often mentioned in interviews the importance of taking their education modules into schools and the group released a more child-friendly version of their iconic video, which had two million views on 13 July 2021 to support their programme. In

February 2022's edition of *When Saturday Comes,* journalist Catherine Etoe focussed on the hard-hitting video to get a sense of the HGT approach to fighting misogyny.

'Launching on FA Cup Final day with a punchy "pass the paper"-style video, the 12 women, kitted out in their respective teams' shirts, each held up a card displaying comments they had received. From the tired "it's a man's game" and "get back to the kitchen" to the intimidating "fancy a shag", it was a powerful 60 seconds that resonated across the sport.'

'The response was crazy; the video got one million views in 24 hours on Twitter,' says Ford. 'And 95 per cent of it was positive – girls getting in touch saying, "thanks and this is my story", dads showing pictures of their daughters, clubs sharing it.'

Another crucial aspect of education is that it may be associated with school and the formative years of young minds, but it is more than a child-centred process. It is a lifelong attitude. For those of any age prepared to listen and find common ground, it structures a self-policing community where shared values dictate the accepted norms and isolate those that break the universally agreed moral codes.

> '*I have never let my schooling interfere with my education.*'
>
> Mark Twain

Writing in Women in Football's Annual Report for 2021, Barclay's group head of sponsorship and media, Tom Corbett, was energised because, where there had been 3,000 schools that offered football to girls two years ago, there were now 10,000. These are tangible markers of progress and describe an exponential growth that mature leagues in England have not seen for decades. But it needs to be underscored by values in the classroom as well as on the pitch.

As I mention later, Barclays Girls' Football School Partnerships leverage schools as a platform with an overarching target of giving girls equal access to football by 2024, a target which is driven by five core principles. A holistic approach of addressing how to make girls more physically active to also help their mental wellbeing is driven by a determination to embed girls' football in secondary schools. By developing and fostering the growth of the women and girls' football workforce there can be real momentum built and oversight created. What chimes perfectly with Her Game Too is the fourth target of making the game inclusive for all. A focus on equality is a much broader base to invite anyone currently marginalised by sex, orientation, religion or disability and collaboration with existing local football providers invites a growth mindset that benefits everyone who loves the game.

This landscape of development and parity, it gives space for other brands and initiatives to start providing more and more opportunities, like Weetabix Wildcats, which gives 5-11-year-old girls a non-competitive environment in which to enjoy games overseen by FA-qualified coaches and volunteers.

'You educate a man; you educate a man. You educate a woman; you educate a generation.'

Brigham Young

The Barclay's Game On campaign also sees the power of education as a delivery system for football to teach wider life skills. PSHE (personal, social, health and economic) education has often been a dry and tedious curriculum. It brings back bad memories as a former secondary school teacher, but this would enthuse and inspire where before it bored and demotivated. All three of Game On's core themes can be energised and clarified when using football for all as a learning point. 'Health and Wellbeing' have the perfect platform when discussing diet, physical and mental health that football develops; 'Relationships' with team-mates, fans, staff and those from other clubs are key life skills in a real context. The third theme, 'Living in the Wider World', is a gift for the global game to show that not only can football – with clubs like Tromso and their QR code-designed kit leading to the Amnesty website or Forest Green Rovers and their bamboo kit – show how the game can educate and sustain, but tournaments like the Women's Euros invite respect, understanding and a chance to learn.

Education is the glue binding the whole of the Her Game Too manifesto together. Through an inclusive and diverse curriculum comes that sense of community with shared values. Research maps out the journey so far but it's also a navigator for the future. With every new story of an inspired, motivated and supported girl comes content to spotlight others as players, staff and fans. HGT content creation to drive the narrative was a huge step forward, allowing HGT to be the primary source of content rather than a secondary receiver of other people's media. One of the first interviews was shared when Everton ambassador Marva Kreel spoke to their England international Izzy Christiansen. This type of interaction not only had the obvious benefits of creating content that promoted the values of the group, but also offered important experience of how to produce and oversee media, expand HGT's network of contacts and showcase its reach and depth. The material helped expand the profile of its YouTube channel as well as offering segmented content for its other rapidly expanding social media platforms. Marva summarised the narrative beautifully with the final paragraph of the piece first published on 11 March 2022.

'Izzy Christiansen is part of a trailblazing generation of women's football, and with her support for Her Game Too alongside her club, she is continuing to pave a way for the next generation of women in sport.'

Stories that emanate from but transcend classrooms build strong profile and relationships with clubs, their trusts and other fans in the local community. The innovative, inclusive approach of Her Game Too's passion for education is that many of its advocates are male voices. The hugely popular merchandising is proudly worn by men to promote their support and further the discussions about parity, respect and opportunity. While too much of football fails to provide for half of any population, HGT taps into the thoughts and support of like-minded people, irrespective of their chromosome count. Writing in the last week of 2021, Mark Little from Phoenix Academy reviewed why he has joined this growing group of value-led companies, clubs and charities that want to partner with Her Game Too. Phoenix's mission statement shows why they are such a good fit:

'Our Mission at Phoenix is to give every child in Wales the opportunity to experience professional coaching to the same level as Elite level football academies delivered in a fun, safe environment for all.'

Mark speaks for many male fans who had previously been cocooned in a hermetically sealed environment of football when he shares a feeling of being educated about casual disenfranchisement and alienation of girls and women that has been allowed to become a self-fulfilling prophecy for women:

'I would say I'm now awake to the problem whereas beforehand I might have shrugged it off. Just like racism and homophobia, we know it's there, but nothing is really done about the problem. So, I'm extremely proud to support this campaign.'

As I mentioned in the preface, there is no line of logic to support selectively respecting women away from the game for their intelligence, strength and experience but to dismiss them when they come in contact with football.

Little continues: 'The logic of sexist hecklers really confuses me. Almost all of these blokes will have a mother. Then the majority will have wives, girlfriends, sisters, aunties and/or daughters. Most of these guys wouldn't dish out the abuse while any of these were present. This just adds to the cowardliness of them. Does it make them feel more manly? I don't know but I don't want to waste too much time trying to understand the minds of these morons.'

The last sentence speaks to the front-foot-forward approach of the Her Game Too team. Education is available to everyone, but people cannot be forced to learn and grow; women should never have to apologise for the shortcomings of men with closed minds.

***

What sets Her Game Too apart from other values-driven organisations is its strong presence at grounds through posters, pitch-side LED screens, merchandise and inside match programmes that also serves to educate those open to fairness and sanction, through reporting systems and self-policing by decent fans, boorish and sexist behaviour. At the start of HGT's campaign, each partner club chose the best way to report misogynistic behaviour but, as the campaign grew, there was a centralised QR code, created in mid-March 2022, that connected directly to the campaign and, if the reporting person was comfortable, the group would raise it with the clubs involved. This centralisation and unity of action was a big step forward. Now Her Game Too was receiving the data directly and getting a more detailed overview of the issues in need of their intervention, support and education.

The presence of Lucy, Caz and other members of the campaign is also an important PR point and validation of the movement's evolving relationships with clubs and fans. It creates a virtuous circle where fans of other clubs petition for inclusion after seeing this intelligent, driven and passionate group of equality advocates visit their clubs (or their rivals). Their personalities advocate for change and leave behind a trail of clubs determined to do their campaign justice.

The hardest environment to educate is the 'wild west' of the www. world. It is the safest place for anonymous and hurtful comments often designed purely to get low-level attention from men who feel hatefulness is better than emptiness. What inspires me about Her Game Too is their forceful refusal to yield. Ignoring is an option to deny lonely misogynists the oxygen of publicity, but they simply won't accept passivity over proactivity. Many of the misogynists flee to newly opened and anonymous accounts, but highlighting their actions makes them serve as unwitting supporters of the equality they profess to hate. Their click-baiting power to shock is neutered by a collective revulsion and forceful repudiation of what underlies their hate speech.

> *'Your admirers make you strong and*
> *courageous. Your detractors make you*
> *successful.'*
> Sanjeev Himachali

In the Her Game Too survey in the appendix, despite the repulsive comments and actions of some mindless males, the respondents also stress the need for education to light the way. Many feel it should be applied equally so that girls see the opportunities that should be offered in an equitable society and boys are educated about how their behaviours (that may be aping those of their parents) have the power to hurt but also to heal. What really appeals to me is that education, by addressing imbalance and unfairness, shares its skills in an even-handed and accessible way without fear or favour. This invites those who will listen to reflect on how diverse thought creates a rising tide of empathy where every vessel on it will float. The survey's 16,000 words of reaction and review are even more remarkable for their lack of anger. The respondents have weaponised kindness that can cause bores to pause rather than fight fire with angry fire. Reading through all the comments, the overriding emotions are sadness, shock and confusion that some men have highly selective arenas of respect for women who could be their sisters, mothers or aunts. For one:

'People are always shocked that I like football and try to catch me out by asking me questions like "what's the offside rule?" or "who is such-and-such?" They aren't major things but they are so sexist and it really, really grates on me.'

For another it is confusion at why she is treated without respect: 'In person, I regularly go to games on my own. I'm always looked at differently. Called "darling", "sweetheart", like "are you lost, darling?" "No. hun, I'm here just the same as you." Even comments like "Oh I didn't think you'd know this much" annoy me cause I'm like "Well why?" My gender shouldn't play a part.'

Being educated needs the barrier of certainty to be lowered and difficult truths to be confronted. Mindless misogyny needs challenging, but it's also important to be open to those who fell onto this point of least resistance in a thoughtless male environment but have taken a choice to change. My wife has no interest in football and her eyes glaze over when I (regularly) mention it. She is exercising her freedom not to support the game, just as the Her Game Too group have made a choice to follow their teams with commitment and passion. If people have to make a choice, education arms them with free will.

> *'Spoon feeding, in the long run, teaches us nothing but the shape of the spoon.'*

> E.M. Forster

10

How the Crouch Report Supports Her Game Too

THERE IS plenty of high-level interest in how Crouch's Fan-Led Review of Football Governance, published in November 2021, helps the journey to parity and inclusion. Barrister Lydia Banerjee, of Lawinsport, expresses clear aims and expectations as part of the Legal Experts' Opinions On The Fan-Led Review Of Football Governance:

'One of the most interesting things about the Review from my perspective is the brief consideration of women's football which comes at Chapter 10. It is striking how the challenges of valuing and growing the women's game have been brought to the fore by the pandemic and the funding issues which arose as revenues were put under pressure. I would be interested to see whether any review if it takes place, looks at the US model, a draft system or any other blue-sky thinking. Growing the game does not need to mean replicating the Premier League, warts and all. It is an opportunity that shouldn't be missed. The call for both parity and a review specifically looking at growing the women's game is made loud and clear. The question for me is whether, without the threat of a European Super League, there will ever be the political and public will to undertake the task.'

The warning signs are there as we wait for the focussed review of the women's game, which Crouch recommended. On

Christmas Eve 2021 Coventry United Ladies FC goalkeeper Olivia Clark shared with her Twitter followers how she and all her team-mates had been released with immediate effect following the club's voluntary liquidation. Coming on the same day that Manchester United offered the potential to build an entirely new stadium purely for their women's team in the league above Coventry, it hit home just how wide the disparity can be for clubs technically close to each other in league standings.

Clark wrote: 'I have no words. To come into work and to find out that you no longer have the job that you've always dreamed of is heartbreaking. Thanks for making me a professional footballer and for the best 2 seasons. The best group of girls you could ask for, Red and Green forever.'

For a club founded nine years ago, that had turned professional in 2021, the decision was mystifying and infuriating in equal measure, especially as it came with no warning for the players and staff who had sacrificed jobs, family time, promotion and security to carve out a professional career in the women's game. Club captain Katie Wilkinson tweeted:

'We had absolutely no indication that the club were in such financial difficulty and it just feels so cruel that at what should be one of the happiest times of the year, our livelihoods, our financial security and our club has been taken away from us just two days before Christmas.'

They were struggling in the Championship after 11 games and one win saw them only above bottom side Watford on goal difference, but that suggests a tricky third season after promotion from the National League South, not an existential crisis from out of thin air. They had struggled to survive in the previous season by finishing second from bottom, five points from relegation and their first Championship season had been even more hazardous, finishing two points above relegated Charlton Athletic. But they survived and, with news in 2021 that Steve Quinlan, Paul Marsh and Darren Langdon had bought a 49 per cent stake in the club, it had seemed as if they had turned the corner.

On 5 January 2022, eight minutes before the deadline for liquidation, the club were saved after an agreement was reached for businessman Lewis Taylor, the founder and managing director of the energy company Energy Angels, to buy the club. But, coming off the back of a fortnight of despair and frustration for the 30 employees, the great news of their survival was tempered by feelings that this should never have been allowed to happen in the first place. It feels like a case study of the warning signs the men's game is experiencing.

Oddly, another club, Derby County, appeared to have been saved in the same week. But, while for The Rams there was clear and brazen financial mismanagement had led them to the edge of the abyss, for Coventry United the environment simply couldn't sustain them and, in some ways, this is even more concerning. At least there was the feel-good factor from, on the potential day of their demise, a Crowdfunder page had raising £15,000 to support them. But, before any of the staff could celebrate, the punishment for mistakes out of their control was handed down to them: a ten-point deduction meant that relegation was highly likely. Of course, this is better than liquidation, but the chances of maintaining a professional operation in the third tier are next to nothing. However, there was to be a karmic finale deep into injury time in the season's final game on 1 May. Needing to beat Watford to survive, they scored the game's only goal in the 97th minute to send the Hornets down through an absolute screamer from outside the box by Mollie Green.

Not only did the temporary demise of Coventry United halfway through a season have grim consequences for the players and staff, it called into question the sustainability of a league only one promotion away from the glamour of the WSL. In response to the situation, the Football Supporters

Association posted the same day how this underlined the imperative need for Crouch's recommended review into the women's game to be instigated without delay.

Guardian writer Suzy Wrack also added a strident and eloquent overview of how this decision could be part of a wider malaise. Tweeting her immediate response, she said she was, 'massively sorry for the horrific situation players and staff at Coventry United find themselves in. To have this happen at any time is appalling, to have it happen two days before Christmas is vicious.'

She then went on to question how a club with such insecure financial fundamentals could have been allowed into the league and the bizarre scenario where a club that decides to turn fully professional is liquidated only months later.

Wrack raised legitimate questions about what due diligence was carried out on the three investors and why there was no meaningful fit and proper test carried out on them. She also shone the spotlight on the lack of support and counselling for the 30 unemployed staff as they started the hunt for another job. Wrack referred to, 'the myth of professionalism and semi-professionalism for those trying to plot careers outside the top WSL table: the reality is professionalism and semi-professionalism are just banners. Fewer than a handful of clubs can afford to provide genuine pro and semi-pro conditions and pay.'

She continued: 'The wages and hours of all outside the very, very top WSL sides are not acceptable, can barely be lived on and do not allow players to build up a safety net.'

In addition, reading the report by the club's insolvency film BK Plus, there remain plenty of questions to answer. No one had been told the month before that the shareholders would not be adding funds to the club and, with BK Plus being instructed 72 hours before liquidation was announced, there seems to have been a rush to judgement; if everyone had been informed, they could have found a solution, or at least bought time to look for one. Coventry United are the poster child for why 'Crouch: The Sequel' needs to be the next taxi off the review rank. Those 30 families and the dreams they temporarily lost deserve nothing less.

***

In a letter to culture secretary Oliver Dowden in July 2021, former sports minister and current MP for Chatham and Aylesford Tracey Crouch highlighted five key areas of the women's game that her report, due to be published later that year, would aim to address:

Growth
Finance flows
Flexibility
Facilities
Diversity.

'The growth and popularity of women's football in recent years is hugely encouraging. However, the Panel has heard much evidence that the sport is now at a critical juncture facing complex and difficult decisions regarding the best approach to take for future stability and growth at both elite and grassroots levels.

'I intend to explore further over the summer how parts of existing finance flows in football to areas such as new or existing transfer and/or agent levies might be more usefully diverted to grow football in the country at the grassroots, amateur, and in the women's game.

'I also believe that there should be consideration of the money flowing into the women's game and exploration of ways that funding can be increased. However, it is more difficult to discern the right model for the future structure of women's football and the evidence from those within the game has been varied. I believe it is crucial to get these issues right before proceeding further, and we will be considering this further over the coming weeks. It is likely that I will recommend that the future of women's football receive its own dedicated review.

'I also consider that the FA should have more flexibility in the use of the money that it generates than it is permitted under the current funding formula which requires an equal split between the professional and amateur games. I strongly believe that this formula should be abolished, and the FA allowed to redistribute its surplus towards the grassroots, amateur and women's game as it sees fit.

'The FA has invested in world-leading facilities for the England teams enabling them to drive forward the positive development of players and success on the pitch. It has also built up the women's game, worked hard to improve diversity including appointing its first female Chair, cooperated closely with Sport England to extend good governance practices to County FAs and continued to invest resources in grassroots football. There is much to celebrate and be proud of.'

When the Crouch Report was released on 24 November 2021, it invited a glass-half-full or empty response. There were 141 references to the women's game across its 162 pages, but a key suggestion was the need for a focussed women's review. The positive spin is to give organisations like Her Game Too and Women in Football time to feed into growing the women's game but, without a date set for starting, it invites the accusation of kicking the can down the road. The way this next step is described as a recommendation and hope that it will 'provide tailored solutions' suggests that those already in the women's game need to do the heavy lifting for some time to come, rather than rely on the current levels of revenue generation. The contract signed with Sky in March 2021 suggests that the revenue streams are starting to flow, but from a low base. This is highlighted early in the Crouch chapter , 'Growing Women's Football':

'Even after the ban on women's football the FA only took direct control of women's football in 1993. Whilst this offered some direction to the sport, the game's development centred on participation growth, rather than commercialisation, spectator support, and media interest.'

The tone of Crouch's overview of the women's game is consistently upbeat, with statements like, 'the strength and depth of the English football pyramid is admired across the globe, and the development of women's football in recent years has been remarkable'. This suggests more concrete policies could have been instigated here to support Caz, Lucy and the Her Game Too group. It cautions the women's game not to make the often-ruinous financial decisions made by the men and focus instead on creating a sustainable model to futureproof the game. However, she also highlights the huge financial imbalances between the men's and women's games that are holding back that hoped-for aim. Crouch points out that the men's FA Cup offered prize money of £16m but that there was only £300,000 for the women's version in the 2020/21 season. For the qualifying rounds alone for the men, there was almost £2m, six times more than the prize money available across the whole of the Women's FA Cup. One contributor to the Crouch report told of how their women's game involved a 260-mile round trip to play a match for which their club received £150, which didn't even cover the cost of the petrol. A match in the same round of the men's FA Cup would have given the winning team £1,800. But, announced in late January 2022, the FA finally decided to materially increase the funds going into the women's FA Cup for the 2022/23 season. By March, more detail emerged about how the prize fund would increase. Although clearly from a disappointingly low base, the almost tenfold increase would see the overall prize pot reach an annual £3m from its previous £309,000. I also really like the idea that the biggest increase in funds will target the cup's early rounds so that those clubs from the lower leagues will get a meaningful financial uplift for competing.

One area that certainly doesn't need to follow in the men's footsteps is the late rearrangement of games to accommodate TV schedules. Two and a half weeks may seem a long time, but for people booking cheaper advance train tickets, hotel rooms and even time off work, this is simply not long enough. As reported by the Football Supporters Association, on 18 January 2022, the fixture between Arsenal and Manchester United on 6 February was changed to kick off at 12.30pm instead of the original 3 o'clock. For the mature men's game, this is unlikely to reduce attendances, but the relatively new women's market is more sensitive to time and date changes. Games shifted to Sundays when public transport becomes scarce are hurting attendances, especially for fans with young families. This thoughtlessness continued for two men's games on 15 May 2022. Everton against Brentford was switched from 2pm to 4.30pm and when West Ham's game with Manchester City was moved from 4.30 to 2pm it meant that the Women's FA Cup Final in Manchester would start at exactly the same time. City fans would be forced to choose between watching the men's or the women's game thanks to the vagaries of Sky Sport scheduling. It was a decision made only 12 days before kick-off.

Another key finding from Crouch was how the arms race of wages and unsustainable spending in the men's game acts as a cautionary tale for the women currently described by her as being at a 'crossroads'. As Mel Morris reflects on the financial carnage he has wreaked on his beloved Derby County, it might give him solace to know that the women's game is determined not to follow in his ruinous footsteps. He has managed to be a cautionary tale, if not a cautious custodian. Overheating wages have already been identified in the women's game. As Kieran Maguire reported in the *Political Quarterly* on 28 December 2021: 'At present, nearly all WSL clubs are losing money and are reliant upon financial support from their holding companies.' This came into sharp relief on 4 March 2022 when Chelsea released their accounts. Even with an income of £5.3m, Chelsea Women lost £1.6m, three times as much as fellow Londoners Tottenham Women. Manchester City Women's 2021 accounts showed losses up from £291,000 to £1.751m. The financial warning lights are now flashing ...

While this is a concern, it is also a positive sign that the overspend is identified in real-time rather than on reflection when standing amongst the smouldering ruins of a once-great club.

Another proactive foreshadowing is the report's concern that women's football will become uncompetitive. If clubs currently linked to the wealthiest men's team dominate women's football the women's game will also make it less commercially attractive to sponsors. With the 2021/2 Women's Super League only containing two clubs, in Reading (an HGT partner club) and relegated Birmingham (who were replaced by Liverpool for the following campaign) with men's teams outside the Premier League, the report worries that the WSL will become too detached from the National Women's League. The concern is also that the Women's Championship, with such rapidly rising riches above, could go the way of the men's version and recklessly mortgage the future for the chance to access the oceans of money becoming available.

The men's game decided on a salary cap for League One and Two by putting an annual wage limit of £2.5m on League One clubs and £1.5m for League Two outfits, in August 2020, but the idea was swiftly ditched half a season later after being found to be 'unconstitutional' by then chief executive of the Professional Footballers' Association (PFA) Gordon Taylor, a man who spent 40 years avoiding his own salary caps as the world's highest-paid union official. For the women's game, the difference between the two top leagues is not only financial. Out of the 12 clubs in the Women's Championship in 2020/21, 11 were registered as part-time, making the leap to playing Chelsea or Arsenal the following season a massive and intimidating prospect. There is already a 'Big Four' of Arsenal, Chelsea, Manchester City and Liverpool who have won all the WSL titles to date, with Arsenal and Chelsea picking up seven of the ten titles competed for so far.

Helping to keep the focus on Tracey Crouch's commitment to a fan-led review of the women's game, in late June 2022, the FSA (Football Supporters Association) published their first survey focussing on it. Running from 7 February to 7 March, 2,156 respondents gave an illuminating snapshot of motivations, frustrations and barriers to entry for women looking to express their love of football. Although a majority of the respondents were female, this was only by a gap of eight per cent, showing the level of enfranchisement men feel in a women's game that has (so far) avoided the tawdry excesses and financial speculation undermining the men's game. Seventy per cent of those taking part supported WSL teams, almost 20 per cent backed Championship clubs and only ten per cent National League clubs and below, showing the huge gaps in resources between the top level and those who aspire to join it. The survey puts a strong faith in Tracey's review of the women's game, as Deborah Dilworth, FSA women's game network manager explained:

'The recently announced independent review into the women's game will be pivotal to a number of these areas of work, and we will strive to ensure that supporters are comprehensively engaged in this process throughout.'

***

Some of the key findings included how '41 per cent said their club should do more on increasing diversity and inclusion' and that, although 'fewer than one per cent of fans reported abusive chants as a major barrier to greater attendance, one in seven (13.9 per cent) responded that they had noticed an increase in the amount of homophobic, racist or sexist language at the match in recent years'.

The survey then fed into a strategy for the women's game for 2022–2024, which had as its central plank an aspect of the men's game that is sadly marginalised. The report feels that, 'supporter engagement is key to the success of women's football' and can be achieved without the use of pernicious Socios (electronic fan tokens to promote fan engagement) or NFTs (non-fungible tokens, which are digital assets representing real-world objects like football shirts or players) to shape the women's game. The second key strategy is for, 'Equality, Diversity and Inclusion to be at the heart of what we do and who we are'.

The findings chime with many of Tracey's conclusions and help to create a groundswell of opinion that, sooner rather than later, there needs to be a report overseen by her, agreed by Parliament that has teeth. The sniping lobbying of Premier League clubs who have tried to hamstring Tracey's report into the men's game will not be an issue here, so the chances of success will surely be higher for the women.

***

Crouch highlights how, with the exponential growth of the women's game, the FA are struggling to keep up and provide adequate levels of officials and infrastructure needed to evolve the game. In some ways, this is a pleasing problem to have. Rather than trying to fan the embers of a game in danger of being extinguished, the Crouch report highlights how the main dangers are caused by an explosion of interest and finance that could cause the problems I saw in Thailand, with the dominance of two clubs drawing on huge resources winning the Thai Premier League title between them for a decade. After rapid growth in the short term, fans walked away from the uncompetitive league, and huge stadiums stand as a cautionary tale against ten years of male hubris.

The route for the women's game is now clear. Look at how the men oversaw their progress and, often, do the opposite. This is something that Tom Vernon, writing in the excellent *Radical Football*, amplifies. For him:

'Women's football is being taken in the wrong direction and that there is an opportunity to change its evolution and build something better, with closer alignment to the original values and interpretation of the game. Inevitably, the game will be successfully commercialised, but it doesn't have to be created in the image of men's football, and perhaps it doesn't even have to be governed by FIFA.'[9]

---

9   Fleming, S. *Radical Football Jürgen Griesbeck and the Story of Football for Good* p. 315, (Pitch Publishing. Kindle Edition).

11.

Why Football Should Remain
a Male-Only Sport

12.

The Power of Parity. Lewes FC

DESPITE THE huge progress being enjoyed by women's football, there remains a reactionary and misogynistic undercurrent to the reaction of some men to women's parity. A study authored by Durham University's Dr Stacey Pope in late January 2022 concluded that over two-thirds of the men polled felt hostile to women's sport in general and football in particular. Using the responses of nearly 2,000 men, the research detected 'openly misogynistic masculinities', across a wide age profile. Most concerning was how the increased openness of some men to women's sport was counterbalanced and overridden by hostility and sexism, suggesting there is a backlash against the increasing parity of women's pay, profile and professionalism.

The study's sample chose the users of message boards. For me, that is taking the temperature of a highly polarising platform. This is an arena where a small number of revolutionaries are kind and supportive, but large tranches of interaction involve a race to the bottom of anger, self-loathing and brainless misogyny.

This was thrown into sharp relief on 13 April 2022 when Her Game Too launched its own podcast, with Caz being interviewed by the show's host Mark Watson. For 90 minutes, we heard frank and harrowing experiences that blight our beautiful game and disgrace the men we allow to wallow in misogyny. Caz highlighted the stomach-turning global issues some women face when joining the male-dominated environment at football matches:

'What we're here to do now is be like "actually we're not okay with this. We don't want to be touched whenever you feel like it and we just want to go and watch the game like everyone else and feel safe and secure".'

She then shared the mental toll that constant abuse and belittling have caused her, from thoughtless online trolls that spill over into the real world beyond their mother's box back bedrooms. For Caz there were troubling health effects:

'I was overcome with anxiety like I even got anxiety in my hands. I've never felt that before. What is that? And I was literally laid in bed and my hands were tingling like a really horrible sensation. I think that's fear overcoming you and that's horrible. When you get a bad feeling you get a horrible feeling that goes all the way through to your stomach.'

This response and the vile actions of a brainless minority have also forced Caz to change her habits and pre-match routines, knowing some of the online abusers are, shockingly, fellow Bristol Rovers fans.

'I've changed pubs now. So, I used to go to the same pub before the game. I used to really love it there but unfortunately, I know they go there now so there is no way I'm going to that pub and it does ruin my actual experience. So, I will not lie and that's the thing. I'm sick of putting a brave face on. I will be honest and say these people will have intimidated me and bullied me and I would not go to the same places as them or actively avoid them. I walked into the first away game of the season at Mansfield with my hood up and hiding my face because I was so worried about these trolls after everything they said about the campaign and me.'

This also led to Caz questioning herself and how people view her:

'I started to really look at myself in a different way and I was really quite upset with how I looked and then I started getting rid of my photos on Instagram as well because I was like, "Oh God. What if they're just going to go through and just like laugh at me or pick out faults with my pictures?"'

Caz then touched on a point made by Laura Woods, mentioned in the preface. The failed logic is that women can be respected across society for their intelligence and insight, but not with football. As Caz described it to Mark:

'If you study to be a vet or if you study to become a teacher you learn these things and it doesn't matter what your gender is. If you're passionate about something you're going to know about it and that is what the Her Game Too girls all are and they all love their football. They have every right to speak about football because they love it.'

For Caz, there is a constant confusion that the abuse she receives often assumes the whole HGT campaign is simply a vehicle for her to increase her profile. 'There's much easier ways I could get attention from men on social media without having to start a national campaign and put my head above the parapet. Trust me, guys.'

There were some positive steps Caz could take and, courageously, she confronted and shared them with her colleagues at work:

'I was brave enough to speak to my work about it the other day which was really quite scary because I don't want them to think that I'm not working my very hardest because I still am, but I wanted them to know that I am getting abusive emails and abusive DMs because I haven't replied to a Her Game Too email within two days. If I'm replying to an email at one o'clock in the morning, I'm then not getting enough sleep to be in the office for nine in the morning and then I'm ultimately falling behind on my day job because my brain is just consumed with Her Game Too stuff. I told them about it and they've been really supportive and we're gonna think of a plan of how I can work around it.'

To help find support for Caz's situation in this often-foetid arena, Pope's study divided the groups into three: progressives (24 per cent), openly misogynists (68 per cent, worryingly) and covertly sexist (eight per cent). The progressives felt highly energised by the increasingly equal access shown by set-piece events like the Women's World Cup, but those openly hostile to women in sport felt they didn't deserve parity, and should be playing more 'feminine' sports. The hidden misogynists were in some ways the worst group of all, professing progressive views in public to mask their dismissive and regressive views privately.

Reflecting on Pope's report, on Sky Sports on 21 January 2022, Lucy Ford shared her opinion that there are:

'People still tweeting sexist comments when a woman decides to have an opinion about a game, whether it's a pundit or a fan or whoever it is in the game. If something happens and people want to Tweet their opinions it's fine, that's what social media is for, for expressing opinions, for a healthy debate about football. But there are still these comments about people being sexist. That misogyny is still rife in football and that's what our campaign's about: to tackle sexism in football across players, fans, background staff, people on the pitch. Everyone in football is affected by sexism.'

The report's co-author John Williams, from Leicester University, said: 'The increase in media coverage of women's sport was openly supported by some men. But it also clearly represents, for others, a visible threat. This is at a time when there are more widespread anxieties circulating among men about how to establish and perform satisfying masculine identities. For men like these, there was a pronounced anti-feminist backlash.'

This is clearly a disturbing finding, but progress is never going to be linear. By highlighting the pull factors to progress, studies like these (and the other influential work authored by Dr Pope) will put us all on guard that, for every step forward, there will be those looking to restrict and destroy the move to equality.

To help provide a more positive and supportive platform, Her Game Too launched their own online forum in February 2022. Open to men and women and moderated to filter out the 'openly misogynists' that Dr Pope referred to, this initiative leveraged the network power of the movement and created a space for supportive and constructive dialogue.

Tweeting on 12 December 2021, Chorley Women FC chair Janet Mitchell said she was left stunned when she faced a £322 bill for the officials in charge of her club's third-round Vitality FA Cup match. As Chorley lost the game 3-0 to Newcastle United, they received £350, but had to fork out for the hire of a 3G pitch due to the poor weather, stomach a defeat and a financial hit for a club already struggling for funds. It not only highlights the nice earner officials are on, but also how the losing third-round men's teams in the Emirates FA Cup receive £1,875, five times as much. As I touched on earlier, the ratio just gets worse with every round. If Chorley had found the magic formula to win the competition, their prize money of £25,000 would have represented 1.4 per cent of the men's £1.8m reward. Staggering.

Lewes FC have come up with two models to support moves being made to address this gross distortion of parity by a values-driven club. The first is a 50/50 split where the £16m pot is split down the middle between the men and women and the other proposal is the prize per fixture approach where both sides of the game would get the same prize money in each round's fixtures. This would only take £4.5m from the men's pot and so would amount to smoother progress to parity. Talking to *Times* journalist Molly Hudson at the end of January 2022, Chelsea Women's manager Emma Hayes added her voice to the incredulity that women get, on average, two per cent of the money in the FA Cup allocated to the men's game. It's not as if the women's game fails to generate the funds needed to pay the players. As Hudson pointed out:

'A crowd of 41,000 attended Chelsea's victory over Arsenal on 5 December, which, even after costs are deducted, would leave a surplus of about £500,000.'

Not only did she describe the current imbalance as 'unbelievable' but Hayes also pointed out that, with more parity, a cup run could have helped clubs like Coventry United avoid their Christmas Eve meltdown. My Exeter City men were essentially saved from extinction by an FA Cup game away to Manchester United in 2005 when they were floundering in the Conference League. They not only shared the gate receipts from the 67,500 fans, but they drew the first leg and a packed St James Park watched their eventual exit. The FA argues that the funds help evolve all levels of the women's game, not only the top. But girls need to have aspirational stories and role models carving out successful careers rather than scraping together the petrol money to barely break even. That is one of the many reasons why Natalie Portman's Angel City FC are so refreshing. As she so stridently shared the week before their first game in March 2022:

'Our dream is to make women's soccer as valued as male soccer is throughout the world.'

Back in England, 100 per cent fan-owned Lewes FC are also cut from a different cloth.

When a club decides to create a level playing field for men and women, it doesn't simply signal their respect for both genders but puts in place an ecosystem that promotes values-driven decisions for all the club's actions. East Sussex's Lewes FC have football's finest stadium name, and The Dripping Pan Stadium houses both the Isthmian League men's team and FA Women's Championship contenders as a setting for dynamic and unapologetic parity. Both teams share the nickname of

The Rooks, but also share meaningful equality in everything they do. In 2017, Lewes became the first professional or semi-professional football club to pay its women's team the same as its men's as part of their Equality FC initiative, but this was just the start. The timing was also telling. We now see full stadiums and a huge profile for the women's game, but this decision was made when it was struggling for the oxygen of publicity. This was the year when the women's season would switch to the winter and supportive structures and strategies were starting to be initiated to help drive the phenomenal growth that the women's game now enjoys. The seeds were just starting to germinate when Lewes made their parity promise. The 2015 and 2016 Women's FA Cup finals both saw record crowds at Wembley, with Arsenal beating Chelsea 1-0 in the latter year in front of 32,912 people.

Speaking just after the decision was made in 2017, Lewes FC director Jacquie Agnew eloquently described how:

'By committing to paying our women's and men's teams equally, and providing equal resource for coaching, training and facilities, we hope to spark a change across the UK that will help put an end to the excuses for why such a deep pay disparity has persisted in our sport. Together with our owners, donors and sponsors, Lewes FC can show that equal pay can be implemented to the benefit of both women and men in sport and beyond.'

Their five non-negotiable aims showed the depth of their pursuit of parity:

1. Raising and setting the playing budgets for the women's and men's first teams at an equal level.

2. Providing equal resource for coaching, performance and strength and conditioning staff.

3. Upgrading equipment and facilities to meet the standards required by higher football divisions.

4. Investment in local grassroots outreach to drive equal participation in football from girls and boys.

5. The club's new campaign, Equality FC, aims to raise awareness about gender inequality in football and encourage more support for women's and girls' football across the UK and around the world.

When I read through their ethos, I see a more focussed version of Bundesliga 2 'Freebooters' FC St Pauli's Guiding Principles. In November 2009 they aimed to create a culture of collaborative and engaging purpose that spoke of their values and aspirations off the pitch. The story since then has not been as rosy. Many of the principles are catch-all commitments to inclusivity, such as 'individuals and groups should subject their present and future conduct to constant self-critical evaluation and be conscious of their responsibility for others'. Their aims are laudable but unfocussed and speak to their determination to be different rather than goal-setting and getting. After 111 years with only eight distant seasons spent in the top-flight Bundesliga, the club is a haven for 'social romantics' seeking solidarity over success.

But, while this approach attracts a gloriously ragtag group of disparate causes coalescing around a similar philosophy of equality in Hamburg, Lewes have refined and defined the approach, to create a highly focussed and consistent manifesto. Their 2021 Club Strategy has five key aims (already ten fewer than their German cousins). The most jarring difference for Lewes is their number one target of 'quality winning football'. St Pauli make no mention of on-pitch success. Indeed, visitors with a silver allergy could comfortably sleep in their trophy cabinet, something the club make a virtue of on a sign in the tumbleweed-filled room: 'We don't have silverware. Instead, we have something a lot better. We have a story to tell. The incredible story of how a community-based club from Hamburg becomes one of the most famous football teams in Europe. Without big trophies. Without big money.'

In fact, for St Pauli, one of the aims of their Guiding Principles is to prepare fans for more trophyless misery:

'FC St. Pauli conveys a way of life and is a symbol of sporting authenticity. This allows people to identify with the club independently of any success it may achieve on the pitch.'

***

Lewes offer clear timelines for their owners around the world (I am proud to count myself as one of them) to measure progress. While St Pauli commit to how 'these principles will form an integral part of contracts and agreements in future and serve as a reference point for everyone involved with the club', Lewes are highly specific:

'This strategy contains the goals, actions and indicators we have been tracking since July 2021, the start of Q3 2021 and continue through the summer of 2022 until we start season 2022/2023. Several of the goals are ongoing, but we will revisit the strategy as part of our season 2022/23 budget development process.'

Lewes's second core target is full financial sustainability, something that is extremely timely in light of Tracey Crouch's Fan-Led Review. Crouch refers to financial sustainability ten times, driven by external, independent regulators. Lewes's self-regulation is a bold and persuasive approach for a grassroots club but there is clearly no appetite for this 'Maoist collective agriculturalism' described by Leeds United's CEO Angus Kinnear in the Premier League. This quote from

Crouch stood out for me to highlight how Lewes are leading the discussion over parity and sustainability:

'Further, the proposed approach seeks, by placing the onus on clubs, to drive good behaviours at clubs by forcing them to think through financial requirements and risk management. It should ensure financial sustainability of clubs, allow for investment and support competition. Unlike other models, it offers clubs significant flexibility.'

The third Lewes manifesto pledge seems rather ramshackle in our world of polished marketing messages but it is endearing and pleasingly self-aware. To Get Their Own House in Order.

The 13 references to women in their strategy are highly specific and actionable. They were aiming for an average attendance of 1,000 fans at men's and women's games by the second quarter of 2022. Leading from their key pillars are specific goals and the first is promotion for both the men's and women's team as a key performance indicator:

'Promotion for both sides would show that a small club that invests equally into both its women's and men's sections can be greater than the sum of its parts. Promotion provides a bigger platform for Lewes FC to prove that a 100 per cent fan-owned club, that is ethically run and forges its own path, can be exemplary on and off the pitch, demonstrating our winning mentality.'

Even more specifically, they have granular targets of average points per game (1.75 for the men and a heady 2.5 for the women). These key actions provide the campaigning platform the club need to address the huge imbalance in FA Cup prize money and to have the financial stability to reject and campaign against 'the gamblification of football', because they are (and this is where I got my credit card out to become an owner) 'always bearing in mind that football has the power to influence wider social norms'.

But, like life at St Pauli, not everything and everyone is harmonious. In 2018, the team were promoted to the FA Women's Championship but in September 2019 club director Barry Collins resigned, frustrated at the board's preoccupation with equality campaigning: 'I joined a football club and feel like I'm leaving a political party.' This chimes with the tensions often evident at St Pauli. Indeed, Nick Davidson's seminal book about the club was called *Pirates, Punks & Politics: FC. St Pauli – Falling in Love with a Radical Football Club*. Welcomed as German football's first openly homosexual president, Cornelius 'Corny' Littmann's reign was controversial not due to his sexuality, but to his focus on sporting and commercial success over and above community engagement.

Ownership Breeds Stewardship

Lewes FC's focus on diversity and inclusion provides the perfect platform for women to write their own stories. Just like me, Maggie Murphy was so inspired by the way Lewes FC do things that she decided to become a member and buy a single share after the club became fully community-owned in 2012. But what she did from there showed just what can be achieved when shared values constructively collide. Talking to *Sussex Living* reporter Sara Whatley in January 2022, Murphy showed how sport can go where politics can't, explaining how 'our choice is whether to use football to bring about changes. We'll get there but we'll get there a lot quicker if we use football.'

She certainly got there quickly. Now the club CEO, Murphy harnesses the drive and experience of a career working in human rights advocacy to drive the club forward.

For Murphy, the eureka moment came in 2017 when the club decided to pay men and women equally and, just as importantly, give both genders equal access to all the club's resources and facilities. This dovetails with the values of Equal

Playing Field, a group she formed to fight for 'Opportunity. Equality. Respect. Nothing more. Nothing less' that fits perfectly not only with Lewes FC but Her Game Too. Like any astute businessperson, she identified the challenges that needed overcoming:

'There were no women involved in decision-making, neither within local clubs nor right up to within FIFA. I've been very active in calling for more diversity in clubs at the decision-making level but also in companies making decisions around what or who to sponsor.'

Her first club role was as general manager for the women's team but, as her brief evolved, two years later she became the club CEO. Drawn to the club's focus on equality, Murphy knows she faces huge challenges in bringing about global parity in the game. As she shared with Whatley:

'We understand that there might be one team in Lesotho that pay their women and men equally, but that's how far you have to go to find another club [doing what we're doing].'

One unintended consequence of a focus on equality was that ticket prices for the women's games have had to be raised annually for the last five years to bring them in line with the cost of watching the men. But, although this may feel jarring to some, it reflects the equal value given to both sides of the club.

The club have a very attractive fan-ownership scheme. Rather like the Trust model used by Exeter City but. This is highly empowering without the need for carpetbagging NFT 'fan engagement' polls featuring fatuous questions. We are owners with real input. Recently, former Chelsea team doctor and Mourinho nemesis (get to the back of the queue) Eva Carneiro became an owner, tweeting:

'Love the beautiful game. Imagine using its power for good. Imagine finding a club with values at the centre of its ethos. Imagine equal pay and equal facility and pitch access for men and women.'

From only £5 a month and without the need for a pernicious Socio NFT, fans are given a share, a vote and access to a new Owner App that lets them give feedback, watch matches live and get merchandise discounts. The different packages are not leveraged to give people with more money higher levels of control but are tiered through an online-only, monthly, annual and lifetime contribution that gives a similar profile and input to the club. These are the type of democratic spin-offs that come when the club truly buys into gender equality. And it works. By January 2022, the club had 2,087 owners from 34 countries:

'I am a Lewes FC Owner because as an American, at first it was the novelty of owning a piece of an English Football club, but I've continued my ownership because I believe in your goals of equality.'

Eric Conduzio

***

In December 2021, *The Times* crowned Lewes FC the Team of The Year. Their chief sports writer Owen Slot praised their pathfinding approach but was left puzzled by how, despite recently signing their biggest sponsorship deal with Lyle and Scott, no other clubs have followed in their footsteps. Commenting on three of their key pillars – equal pay for both genders, complete fan ownership and no betting advertising – slot is unequivocal. 'It's about bloody time.' Roger that from me.

***

In the wider game, pay parity is starting to gain momentum from its unequal base. In fact, in early June 2022, it even tipped over into a different type of disparity. The Canadian men's team boycotted training for their game against Panama on 5 June (leading to its cancellation) in protest at their level of compensation when compared to women players. Having qualified for the World Cup for the first time since 1986, the men's team were demanding a 40 per cent cut of the nation's tournament earnings, but had been offered only ten. Looking south of the border, Canadian players could see how the US Soccer Federation's decision to share over 80 per cent of their World Cup revenue equally between male and female players had caused peace to break out.

The Canadian men demanded equality with the Olympic gold medallist women's team and it seemed odd that, in a time of unprecedented success for Canadian national teams, there was claim and counterclaim of he-said, she-said rather than the feeling of parity and equity that seems to have been negotiated amongst their southern neighbours.

***

When a YouGov survey in January 2018 asked whether the general workforce should enforce the gender equality pay approach of north European country Iceland, 70 per cent agreed it was the right thing to do, with 78 per cent of women and 62 per cent of men agreeing. A year later, in March 2019, YouGov asked women and men if they thought more needed doing to reach gender equality. This time 71 per cent of respondents felt there was still some way to go, with 80 per cent of women and 62 per cent of men agreeing. By August 2021, responses to the question, 'Do Brits personally think gender equality has been achieved in relation to equal pay?' only 24 per cent felt it had been achieved in the wider workforce. On International Womens' Day 2022, YouGov published a survey showing how, over the last decade, Britons have become much less satisfied with how women have been treated in society. In the general population, the percentage of people who are satisfied has dropped from 71 to 50 per cent whilse the number of people dissatisfied has risen from 22 to 41 per cent.

The specious argument that women in football deserve less pay than men because they don't generate the same revenue perpetuates a vicious circle of low pay and profile leading to limited opportunity instead of the virtuous one highlighted by *The Guardian*'s Suzanne Wrack in October 2019. In the small town of Burlington, Vermont, players and fans alike were inspired by the chants of 'equal pay!' ringing out in Stade de Lyon three months earlier after the USA women's national team lifted the World Cup trophy with a 2-0 victory over the Netherlands. A member of the crowd that day, Helen Worden, scored a late winner for her high school against South Burlington and her response set a chain of events in motion that spotlighted how the time is right for equal pay. The team had planned to all lift their shirts to reveal '#equalpay' on their undershirts but, in the moment, only four players remembered. They were all booked, an action that became a key focus for the campaign that followed. This inspired the crowd to start their own chant of 'equal pay!', which put in train an online campaign that attracted support from their local senator, Brandi Chastain, Mia Hamm and even Billie Jean King, and that fed into the Change the Story campaign to improve women's economic security in the state. And, as Wrack explains, the story has only just begun:

'Looking to broaden the conversation and capitalise on the momentum, they are distributing yellow cards with shirts and have set up in the school cafeteria to encourage people to write down what cause 'they would take a yellow card for' and asking them to photograph themselves and use the hashtag #excessivecelebration'.

Nearer to home, the Welsh FA has committed to gender-equal pay for their national teams by 2026. Looking to break through the 'grass ceiling', the Irish FA has already introduced gender pay parity for its national teams, which was achieved

Her Game Too

by a combination of the male players agreeing to a pay cut matched by the FA. Wales and Ireland join England, Brazil, Australia, Norway and New Zealand, who have equal pay agreements with men's and women's teams. The figures are in some ways symbolic (the English men's team give their appearance money away to charity and it clearly only relates to the tiny percentage of players that make the national team grade) but it sets an important precedent and feeds into the discussion of how equal pay breeds increased respect.

For many observers, the highly effective 'equal play, equal pay' campaign by the USA women's national team was a template for how to get results both on and off the pitch. In 2019, after three fruitless years of demanding equality, in 2019 they took their own federation to court to pursue better pay and conditions. The campaign was epitomised by its spokesperson in Megan Rapinoe and her front-foot-forward approach to negotiating. She even persuaded the US team to wear their shirts inside out to protest about unequal pay between men and women. In her *New York Times* bestseller book *One Life*, she describes how:

'Nothing spins my wheels like an unfair fight, and the same goes for [her sister] Rachael. We're not looking for an altercation, but we're not going to back down from what's right.'[10]

The beauty of the American women's approach is that it came from a place of rightful entitlement rather than gratitude. They knew their worth and were determined to be rewarded accordingly rather than accept that, despite their serial successes, they would be given the bare minimum pay and conditions. Their argument's headlines focussed on their remuneration, but it is the precarious nature of women choosing football as a career with heartbreaking situations

---

10 Rapinoe, M., Brockes, E. *One Life*, (Penguin Publishing Group. Kindle Edition, 2020-11-09T22:58:59).

like the Coventry United Ladies FC that need attention. These ferociously driven winners knew that, by continuing to dominate the Women's World Cup, their story simply wouldn't fade away and could also be used as leverage in their long battle against their own association.

'[Winning the World Cup] is huge,' Rapinoe said. 'We've been shy to say that and put so much pressure on ourselves because we think we have a case no matter what. But this just blows it out of the water. Is it even about that anymore, or is it just about doing the right thing? The Federation is in a unique position to ride this wave of good fortune.'

These women know that, to get a seat at the decision-making tables, winning is not enough. They also need to sweat the dollar signs. Since winning the 2015 World Cup, they have generated game revenue of $50.8m, a figure the men's team can't match.

The argument is more nuanced than victories and cash flows in the American sporting landscape however. There is a consistent background of gender equity being part of the American way of supporting grassroots girls to flourish and become today's superstars. That focus on equity also shows in their draft and roster system which, like its counterparts for men, rewards weaker teams with prize draft picks for the next season. This is anathema for many UK fans in the men's game, but it's an approach that nurtures early-stage leagues and helps smooth out huge disparities in resources that lead to too many lopsided contests that damage a league or a competition's brand value. It also guards against stockpiling the best players in a jealously guarded cabal of top clubs that starve others of talent, even if they have no room for them in their own team.

Women players in USA teams have the advantage of a highly evolved system of collegiate pathways. My local team, Exeter City Women, have a productive pathway system leading from the local Exeter College that feeds into their development team to provide a talent pool for the first team, but this is a process taken on at their cost and by diverting resources to the process. America's 'pipelining' approach began to bear fruit on 2 February 2022 when US Soccer and women's players settled an equal pay lawsuit that had been rumbling on for six years. Under the terms of the agreement, the athletes will receive $24m and a promise from the federation for pay parity in men's and women's national teams. This took huge perseverance from the World Cup-winning United States women's team but has now created a pathway for girls and women to forge meaningful and realistically remunerated careers in the game.

But the American system is not only a refined process of player development. They also know that the product needs constant evolution and revolution to capture the attention of a customer base bombarded with other sports to fill their leisure time with. Two new teams entering the NWSL 2022/23 season may have been invited rather than promoted, but rather than being a West Brom or Norwich yoyo team, they come in highly resourced and with eye-catching talent. Angel City include new signing and World Cup-winner, Christen Press, while San Diego Wave are coached by former Manchester United manager, Casey Stoney. The 2023 Super League will also create the aspirational environment that drives development and is expected to double the number of professional women's teams.

Follow the Angels?

Jarringly for English ears, before kicking a ball, Angel City described themselves as 'a brand on a mission to make a difference in this world'. 'As opposed to other planets?' a cynic might reply. But there is plenty to listen to and learn from with their project. Backed by the uber stylish Hollywood A-lister Natalie Portman and a network of smart, majority female and high-profile figures, including technology venture capitalist Kara Nortman, media and gaming entrepreneur Julie Uhrman and tech entrepreneur and venture capitalist Alexis Ohanian, they have a 22,000 capacity Banc of California Stadium in Los Angeles shared with MLS Western Conference club side Los Angeles FC as their platform.

They astutely signed up Women's Sports Group founder and FA advisor Dame Heather Rabbatts to extend their reach globally, using their three core competencies of, 'strategic communications counsel, media rights management and partnership development'.

'The club's innovative approach is already resonating hugely with football fans, and we're excited to be working with them to bring their global vision to life,' said Rabbatts.

The kit, made from recycled materials, was designed by the fans and they secured the biggest shirt sponsorship in the NWSL with Deliveroo. The club have circumvented the idea of building slow and strong, which may also jar English ears, but they have the chutzpah to aim big with a franchise system that gives them direct access to the top league.

There is plenty to learn from across the pond for our women's game here. The warning signs are flashing that Chelsea, Arsenal and Manchester City have pooled such vast resources they are likely to continue their domination of the game after filling the top three slots for the last half-decade. But, with its equitable approach, the women's game can be confident that decisions made will aim to foster parity and collegiality over dominance and the turgid processions we see in so many male European leagues.

13.

Our Manifesto: Awareness.

TWO OF the key drivers for Her Game Too's meteoric rise are the personalities and indefatigable energy of founders Caz May and Lucy Ford. They have driven interest through a huge range of initiatives but have also made themselves available for media focus to get their message eloquently across. When talking to the BBC's Sophie Hurcom in September 2021, Caz and Lucy laid out why they set up the movement. For Lucy, it was driven by the appalling reaction she received as a young female football fan:

'I've had it [abuse] since I was in secondary school. I've been a big football fan since I was ten years old and I've had it in school where guys and even teachers would say to me "Why are you a football fan, why are you spending your weekends doing that?"'

The catalyst for setting up Her Game Too was a survey conducted in early 2021 which had almost 400 respondents. They related stories of being patronised, questioned, harassed and intimidated just for being a female football fan. I have put the full survey and all the comments they received in the appendix. I was very tempted not to include some of the appalling things my gender stoops to when describing women, but I decided that you need to see them. Be warned: you will want to take a bath in Clorox afterwards. This appalling

Celebrating the HGT first anniversary with my wife Karen. Castlav Nekic

Caz and Lucy's proud parents. Castlav Nekic

Caz May enjoying HGT's anniversary. Castlav Nekic

Castlav Nekic

Castlav Nekic

Megz from We Love Sport *filming HGT's anniversary.* Castlav Nekic

Castlav Nekic   Castlav Nekic

Calum Best is a huge supporter of the women's game. Castlav Nekic

Castlav Nekic   *It's been a real team effort.* Castlav Nekic

Companies like NI Mugs have helped spread the word. Scott Gordon

We all need to be more like Marie.

A pleasure to meet. Nationwide's Chris Hull

Helen Nkwocha. A true pathfinder.

Castlav Nekic

Castlav Nekic

Castlav Nekic

Start Her Young.
A. Mitchell

Stronger Together. Neill Richardson @Falselights15

Neill
Richardson @
Falselights15

Winners. Neill Richardson @Falselights15

*Proud to
sponsor Zoe
Watkins.*

Only one winner.

Calm authority.

Professor Denise Barrett-Baxendale MBE.

Hayes the trailblazer.

It's Her Game Too.

All aboard the 'banter' bus.

Bring out the Best in men.

situation was retold movingly by journalist Caoimhe O'Neill in her article for *The Athletic* in July 2021, in which she reflected on her experiences during the Euros:

'Do you want to know why I was scared walking through the crowd of England fans? I was scared I was going to get touched or grabbed inappropriately. Just as verbal abuse will ring in your ears, once somebody has fondled you, you never quite forget what that unwanted transfer of energy feels like.'

Fortunately, Adam Tutton and his colleagues at Bristol Rovers Community Trust read and responded to the upsetting stories being shared. As Tutton related to the BBC:

'When the girls brought that to our attention, I think all of us at the community trust and at the football club were really, really shocked and felt we needed to do all we could to support them.'

For Lucy, the astonishing take-up of the Her Game Too movement is proof positive that there was (and is) a desperate need for girls and women to have a listening ear and a proactive approach to a universal challenge for women in the game. While Her Game Too is not the only community looking to address the insidious imbalance across the sport, they are one of the most fan- and club-facing groups whose match-day visibility is expressed loud and proud across a growing range of stadiums in all four professional leagues and a broad range of non-league organisations.

Despite every opportunity to be dragged down by the misogynistic pushback they receive, they have decided to weaponise kindness.

> *'Never argue with an idiot. They'll drag*
> *you down to their level and beat you*
> *through experience.'*
>
> Mark Twain

Before meaningful action must come awareness and Her Game Too has created a compelling range of ways in which to engage and inform the widest possible audience. Clubs have promoted the campaign through pitch-side advertising boards, selling merchandise in their souvenir shops, and putting posters around their grounds promoting the partnerships. Merchandise acts as another aspect of HGT's soft power and evolved from HGT-focussed apparel to joint ventures between them and clubs. One of the first to make the next step was Wigan Athletic who, in early May 2022, launched their Laticsx@HerGameToo Range that stylishly combined the crest of the club and the campaign.

Her Game Too energises shirts as catalysts for meaningful change as a key part of their culture. Caz, Lucy and the team have taken a front-foot, fan-centred approach to spread the message of inclusion, respect and tolerance with their logo embossed on shirts across the UK acting as vibrant calling cards. In their famous YouTube video, each of the 12 founding members wears the shirt of their favourite clubs while holding up misogynistic comments often brainlessly tossed in their direction at matches. This creatively illustrates how the country's most powerful clubs try to act as if all fans are welcome, but often fail to enforce or support meaningful inclusion.

Incredible groups promoting tolerance like Women in Football and the Gay Football Supporters' Network are making real progress, but the way HGT has harnessed the power of our clubs' shirts has been their unique selling point. At Exeter City, during October 2021's Her Game Too Weekend, the men's and women's teams warmed up in Her Game Too shirts while the logo was proudly displayed on electronic perimeter advertising hoardings. Since then, the campaign has forged partnerships with Everton, Leeds United and Brentford as well as over 100 other clubs where shirts carry the message of respect for women.

Whether it is on a local women's team kit or in partnerships with much higher-profile clubs like Everton, club shirts have served as a defiant delivery system for Caz, Lucy and the group's message that sanitises the fabric from foetid and unregulated pseudo gambling schemes. But they took this one stunning step further. In October 2021 they launched their own shirts through a bespoke manufacturer Hope and Glory (every shirt is made for individual orders). Their agreement with HGT was forged in a spirit of mutual support between two empathetic groups and lay the groundwork for increasing future opportunities. Talking to Caz about it, she told me this was very much a partnership based on shared values:

'They are donating 100 per cent of the profits to us, which we can then donate towards the development of grassroots girls' football. It's not much advantage for them except it gives them a bit more exposure as a company. But they are mainly doing it because they support the message of Her Game Too.'

One of the first products was a hoodie that Calum Best can often be seen rocking, and a black T-shirt, but a new addition in October 2021 really raised the bar and greatly increased awareness. The Her Game Too football shirt has been a huge hit across the board. With a much lower price-point than men's football shirts, which often go for £70 in the Premier League, not only does this only cost £30 but is made to order and all proceeds go to grassroots women's football. This means that, rather than financing Jeff Bezos's next trip into space, the customers are empowered by making tangible change for a movement they passionately believe in, bringing a sense of enfranchisement and ownership.

During 2022, the merchandising kicked into a higher gear. Not only could you get a range of polo shirts, T-shirts, hoodies, hooddresses and zoods (I had to look them up too) but also baseball caps, bobble hats and baby wear. In January 2022, knowing that some fans were struggling for funds, stepped payments were introduced, with three monthly, interest-free instalments after a small deposit. Hope and Glory stressed that HGT would receive the same donation and upfront payment for every item, cementing their position as a trusted and ethical partner.

When I spoke to Ric Dennis from Hope and Glory, he was enthused and inspired by the way his merchandise had been shared and received. And it's not only the take-up that has been amazing. Chris from @chatshirt rated the Her Game Too football shirt design the best of 2021. The shirt not only sends out a powerful and timely message but does it in an achingly stylish way.

As Chris describes it, 'this shirt is fantastic: sleek and understated, the little yellow flag details popping in the material, everything you'd expect from one of the best shirt suppliers out there at the moment. Hope and Glory, who on the day this video is coming out are still taking orders for the next one of these shirts by the way people, and with Everton being one of the most recent clubs to get behind this fantastic cause, it really seems that 2022 is going to be the year of Her Game Too.'

So now there is a neural network of HGT shirts amplifying partnerships with a broad range of clubs, driving an irresistible narrative passionately endorsed by players, fans, commentators and administrators. With their dynamic social media presence, every shirt is a platform for a personal statement that weaponises kindness and tolerance. These stories take on a collegial, compelling life of their own as they navigate narrative networks to weave a tapestry of shared experience.

For HGT there are also innovative tactics like a partnership with @mrflag , which is running a competition to design a logo for 6ftx4ft rainbow flags, with the winning designer getting a free art service and flag. This is part of a highly effective 'nudge theory' of regular influence points.

One seemingly small but helpful initiative was that on 4 March 2022, to help celebrate the partnership with Oxford United, the pre-match playlist would be made of empowering songs celebrating women. Hearing female voices around the ground also nudges inclusion in more subtle ways. Even Ozzie the Owl, Sheffield Wednesday's mascot, proudly wore an outsized HGT shirt around Hillsborough for their 6-0 demolition of Cambridge United on 12 March. Reading's captain Natasha Harding wore her armband featuring the Her Game Too logo for their game against Manchester United and a carnival band walking and playing as they headed to Goodison Park were all proudly wearing HGT T-shirts on the same day.

Newport County had a female stadium announcer on 5 March as part of their Her Game Too dedicated fixture and, by all accounts, Niamh smashed it. Adding to the 'you can't be what you can't see' mantra, what you hear also helps to constructively shape perspectives. A consistent interaction online with like-minded supporters also reaches out to similarly open-minded football fans like the huge LGBTQ+ network.

One of the most eye-catching ways Caz, Lucy and the group have spread awareness is by selecting values-driven partners like Hope and Glory. To celebrate making them their official apparel partner on 7 January 2022, HGT was able to scale-up the competitions they created and the prizes on offer. The high-profile club connections also allowed it to offer unique prizes that not only drove even more traffic through its channels but created the 'halo effect' of placing the club and all they stand for next to HGT and what it represents. Brentford offered a Her Game Too T-shirt signed by all the players in May 2022. To win, people needed to follow Her Game Too Brentford FC and tag a friend. The scale, reach and momentum of HGT meant it was now creating a virtuous circle for itself and its allies, underpinned by trust and common purpose.

There was also an entire Her Game Too kit set for clubs in a range of colours that would not only create increased attention and participation and raise profile for the lucky club keen to spread the message further and wider.

Merchandise encourages an empowering, inclusive and open-source approach to supporting the Her Game Too campaign. In addition to leveraging kits, it also opens the door to niche and committed creators to add their voices to the discussion that diffuses the narrative across mainstream and specialised channels. One example is Dave from Cross Stitch Shirts (@X_Stitch_Shirts), who has created a stunning range of bespoke, complex miniature designs for cross-stitching fans to complete. It also pays homage to the Her Game Too shirt that adds more traction to the idea that this is a broad-based movement across gender, orientation, class and race. If you want fairness and a fair shake for women in football you are welcomed without question, fear or favour.

***

Her Game Too's spirit of bold innovation just kept expanding exponentially. In February 2022 it partnered with *FAWSL Full-Time*, a monthly magazine chronicling all the stories from Women's Super League and Women's Championship club.

For those with a lower price point in mind, there is even an HGT mug from Nimug.com that is sold both online and in some of the smaller club souvenir shops. When I talk to Ric from Hope and Glory and Scott from Ni Mug, they feel enthused and inspired by the way their products are shared and received. Ric told me:

'The response to the HGT garments has been great – similar to when we launch new items for our partner clubs, but the take-up with HGT has been amazing.'

But most of all, the money they are helping to generate will be folded back into the development of grassroots women's football with a focus on sustainability. For Ric:

'We go about things in a slightly different way to other small brands. We pride ourselves on quality and design and also have strong sustainable beliefs.'

You don't get that buzz from Amazon when your OLAPLEX Hair Perfector No.3 Repairing Treatment drops onto your doormat …

***

But the strategy for brand awareness and support for the grassroots game was more than 'merch' sales. There were (#HERGAMETOO & Adidas Predator Mutator 20+) boots on the ground in the shape of 25 (and rapidly rising) club ambassadors. From Marva at Premier League partners Everton across the leagues to Emily at Championship Birmingham City, Abbie at League One Rotherham and Izzy at League Two Newport County, all levels of the professional game had an HGT ambassador as a link, catalyst and role model. Much of the work was to forge and further partnerships with clubs, but there was also awareness work to be done. This role became so wide-ranging that, in early 2022, advocates were introduced who would support them and help with both club and community communications. For example, on 6 March 2022, HGT volunteers were at the Reading against Spurs women's game handing out flyers and posters to keep the connections active.

There was also ambassadorial innovation in late February 2022 when the campaign announced its first gaming ambassador. @SophRicho, with over 50,000 Twitter followers, was tasked with driving the HGT message home across global tournaments in an innovative, eye-catching and strategic way to draw in even more 'eyeballs' to the cause. These high-energy partners also gave access to increasingly broad platforms to turbocharge their virtuous circle. On 4 March 2022, JD Football's blog shared with its 28,000 followers how Her Game Too was 'Moving Football

Forwards'. They gave an insight into how the campaign ticks and its key targets, but also demonstrated how the campaign has become increasingly attractive to corporate partners who want to associate themselves with such a values-led campaign, something Chris Hull touched on in our interview.

On the eve of the HGT first anniversary, big brands were picking up on the opportunities an association with HGT can create, supported by figures like those released on 5 May, 2022, by Sky Sports, which reported that 17.9 million people watched women's sports up to April 2022, compared with 6.7 million at the same stage in 2021. As part of a new campaign, Fresher Football, Heineken produced a set of Champions League statistics without gender bias to challenge football stereotypes. It was supported by a bold and stylish ad with the intriguing strapline of 'Cheers to all fans. Men included'. This strident, uber-confident approach fits seamlessly into the HGT ethos. Cleverly, the marketing team at Heineken knows that stats are not gender dependent. All progress is hard-won, from the Premier to the Isthmian League, in the WSL or West Riding WFL Division 3. Backed by their multi-year sponsorship deal with the UEFA Women's Champions League and UEFA Women's Euros, creating gender-neutral stats immediately creates a huge new market for the product and a way to start opening doors for the previously closed shop of men-only stats. Not surprisingly given Heineken's investment, the Fresher Football stats focus on the UEFA Champions League with categories like top goal-scorers and most successful teams irrespective of gender. The hope is that this campaign will prove to be the vanguard rather than an outlier.

These good news stories have been gaining huge traction. On 30 October 2021 Talksport shared with its 1.6 million listeners an interview with Caz and Lucy highlighting the incredible job they are doing and the forces ranged against them. In discussion with reporter Natasha Everitt, they highlighted why they felt they had to act. When reflecting on the depressing results from the HGT survey that found almost 92 per cent of the surveyed women had witnessed online sexist abuse aimed at women, Everitt said:

'And these figures don't lie – the hate towards women in the game is still much more common than people think and the campaign has clearly struck a chord with women across football.'

The data they collected was supported the following month when the Football Supporters Association released their survey concluding that a stunning one in five women had been subject to unwanted physical attention at a match and almost half of the 2,000 respondents felt angry when witnessing sexist behaviour at games. Some hopeful news for Caz and the team was that now only four per cent compared to ten per cent of women in 2014 feel that sexism is just part of a match-day experience and the amount of women who laugh off this type of behaviour has halved from 24 per cent to 12.

As I touched on earlier, another, long-term arena for creating inclusion for future fans and players is going into local primary schools to educate children about Her Game Too, which will lay the groundwork for seeing inclusion as the norm rather than the exception.

The need for education was perfectly illustrated not only by an astonishing misogynistic outburst from former footballer David Speedy, but by the way he was reached out to rather than ostracised after his moronic comments. On 16 October 2021 as part of the commentary team for his former club Coventry City (now a Her Game Too partner club) as they prepared to take on Blackburn Rovers, Speedy offered how 'too many women' pundits are 'spoiling men's football'. He was chastised by fellow commentator Clive Eakin who highlighted the idiocy of what Speedy had just said by clarifying:

'We don't endorse those views at all. Frankly, women have added a great deal to our media coverage of football, and it's not before time.'

Speedy suffered heaps of online abuse for his views and it would have been easy to consign him to the bin of sexist bores, but then Women in Football CEO Jane Purdon contacted him with a conciliatory approach. This was a mature and productive move by Jane, giving time for Speedy to reflect on his actions and learn more about himself rather than ostracising and radicalising him. He tweeted, two days after his outburst.:

'I'd like to thank @WomeninFootball CEO Jane Purdon for reaching out to me today. In what's been a difficult 24/48 hours, she showed care and compassion towards me. I am hopeful we can start a positive conversation on the impact women have made and are making in football.'

A classy end to a sorry-starting affair.

***

It is not only individuals who show themselves to be in need of enlightenment – some football clubs are still in the same boat. A month after Her Game Too was established, Norwich City, with their female owner, took a stunning misstep to show just why the work of Caz, Lucy and the team is so important. Signing a £5m deal with Asia-focussed casino BK8 (routed through Malta of course) seemed like just another tawdry tip towards shirts being delivery systems to get around gambling laws in countries like Thailand where, technically, it is illegal. But due diligence is a powerful thing, especially when you choose not to do it. Not only was this a company leveraging football for monetised misery by using white label (or 'ghostship') companies and complex financial structures (which we all do when we have nothing to hide) but they also specialised in bizarre erotic services in Malaysia including 'sexy baccarat' and, gulp, suggestive hot dog swallowing contests. Norwich supporters coalesced around #hergametoo and, to the club's credit, they cancelled the contract swiftly. But it's stunning that this was ever allowed to happen. Being blinded by the size of a cheque is no excuse for being deaf to what makes an ethical partnership that your team shirt legitimises.

Just when we hoped this would be a lesson in doing your homework before collecting the cheque, at the end of 2021 BK8 became the official global betting partner of Huddersfield Town. You have to wonder what the Town fans have done to deserve Paddy Power mocking them and now being Norwich City's cast-off patsies. But this murky agreement is just one symptom of a much wider malaise.

***

Back to the positives, to partnerships that have helped to cast the Her Game Too net further and wider. Working together with awards-makers Awards FC, HGT offer monthly trophies to those people who help further the cause of women's football. Launched in March 2021, the first recipients were at the Gashead twins' beloved Bristol Rovers. Their Women's FC chairman Adam Tutton and co-founder Matthew Davies were rewarded for their fight against misogyny in the beautiful game.

Talking to the Bristol Rovers Women's FC website, Awards FC praised the duo, saying:

'Their hard work in the fight for equality and inclusion in football has not gone unnoticed. The team at Her Game Too has spoken very highly of all they have done so far. We thank them for being dedicated advocates of this cause.'

Davies added: 'Myself, Adam and everyone involved with Bristol Rovers Women's FC are honoured to be the first-ever recipients of the 'Her Game Too Hero Award'. We pride ourselves on being an inclusive, community-based football club who believe that all participants and supporters should be respected, regardless of gender or any demographic. We've all witnessed the sexist abuse that females in football have received online and in person, so we knew that this was a campaign that we needed to support. We can't wait to work with the team on further projects in the near future.'

This creative approach to bringing HGT, Awards FC and clubs together has reaped rich rewards, creating heart-warming stories that further stoke the fires of their social media platform and ever-growing list of well-wishers and active supporters.

This partnership proved to be so successful that, on 1 April 2022, Awards FC launched its own Her Game Too range on its website. Now clubs and associations can source medals, trophies and player-of-the-match lanyards. Every purchase not only strengthens the partnership, but pushes the HGT brand further out into the footballing world. A classic case of enlightened self-interest.

***

Each of these influence points keeps the logo and story of Her Game Too in the public eye at the centre of commendable campaigns, but there is also another highly effective way for the HGT message to be embedded in people's minds. For its next edition, *Football Manager* will have the Her Game Too ads as one of the chosen pitch-side sponsors. This is something incredibly high profile and profoundly important as a way of adding gender equality debates to the mainstream rather than the margins. But, as importantly, it makes one step forward to football being just … football. As Adrian Durham commented on his Talksport show in October 2021:

'Just love football. Just love the game. It doesn't matter who's playing it, does it?'

It's also something 2021 FIFA Women's coach of the year Emma Hayes feels extremely passionate about. Talking to *The Athletic*'s Iain Macintosh in July 2021, she pulled no punches about *Football Manager*'s decision to include women's games on their platform for the 2021/22 season:

'That's how you change culture, with huge moves like [that].'

Macintosh amplifies how the 'announcement is a literal game-changer. This isn't just a simple data update; this is going to be a painstakingly-produced simulation of the women's game from grassroots to the international scene and Hayes does not doubt what it means.'

Supporting Hayes's insistence that the online universe needs to tackle misogyny head on, in early February 2022, Her Game Too became official partners with ECL Gaming to create more female gaming ambassadors like @SophRicho for the platform to help drive the movement towards equality, diversity and inclusion. Björn Rüssel, COO of Rush.gg, the platform ECL added: 'We are proud to have partnered up with ECL and Her Game Too. We are driven by our belief, that all gamers are equal and that there is no place for any form of sexism, racism or hatred, neither in real life nor in gaming and esports.'

Monthly community cups inviting women within *FIFA 22* to create their own FIFA tournaments and provide industry experience of operational aspects of gaming and esports will be supported by a talent competition to run parallel to the events, helping uncover female FIFA content-creators and streamers, forging more pathways for girls in the esports and gaming space.

***

A ringing endorsement of how Hayes goes about her business as coach and pundit came on 4 November 2021 when she was voted Pundit of the Year at the Broadcast Sports Awards thanks to her Euro 2020 coverage that showcased her incredible preparation, insight and passion for the game. Not only is this an astonishing achievement, but it fosters the idea that excellence does not need to be categorised by gender.

Hayes's incredible standing across the game as an eloquent, passionate advocate of equality was further rewarded on 25 May 2022, when she was named the FA WSL Manager of the Season after Chelsea's third consecutive title under her watch; her team scored 62 goals and conceded only 11. In a season when The Blues also lifted the Vitality Women's FA Cup, Hayes cemented her voice as key to the conversations about equal access to the beautiful game across genders and platforms.

Like Exeter City's Her Game Too Weekend in October 2021, *Football Manager* is creating a conversational parity where players are great or terrible based only on what your thumbs do and not the chromosomes of the person playing. The conversation will be normalised rather than polarised through sexist prisms. There is also now strident confidence when major corporations create playing parity between the genders. Sports Interactive's studio director Miles Jacobson told Macintosh:

'I've got a really simple message for people,' he said. 'If you don't like what we're doing, don't play our game. If somebody thinks that putting women's football in *Football Manager* is going to ruin their experience, well, I'm sorry. Don't play our game anymore. We don't need that money.'

Hayes rounds off the conversation with a rallying cry that has been taken up by Caz and her crew as she projects into the future:

'But I think about my nieces and nephews. They're being brought up in very different gaming cultures. You think maybe in ten years' time, they could be playing *Football Manager* with their mates and it's not even a conversation whether Emma Hayes is managing Liverpool or Man United … And so it has to start somewhere. That's how you change culture, with huge moves like this.'

And these moves are creating meaningful traction already. At the beginning of May 2022, National League North club Chester City chose a new general manager from the 90 applications, after interviewing five. One of the interviewees showed a particularly strong skill set with a focus on maximising efficiencies and club revenues through experience, ability and personal charm. The other attribute the chosen person had was that of being a woman. Georgina Slawinski had the type of pedigree, qualifications and experience that a non-league club would rarely have access to, including first-class honours in sports business and coaching from UCFB Wembley and a master's degree in Football Business at the Football Business Academy. As Chester's director described her:

'Georgina blew the panel away with her passion and knowledge for football and sports business and had done extensive research on Chester FC whilst having a specific plan on how she would help move the club forwards broken down into four sections of prestart, 30 days, 60 days, and 90 days.'

Rather than an outlier, Chester City are a vanguard club that knows how much talent is out there if they review a CV for content over chromosomes.

***

With a rapidly increasing profile and spreading network of awareness, the indomitable dozen at HGT have, in less than a year, moved from asking if people would support these developments to 'Why wouldn't you?' Emma Hayes must be very proud. Before joining Harry Redknapp as assistant coach for a Soccer Aid charity match, Emma spoke to *The Athletic* journalist Sarah Shephard after yet another stellar season with Chelsea. The article, published on 11 June, showcased the passion that we all feel for the game, regardless of age, orientation or chromosome count:

'Football is ... Everything. Everything and more. It's my love, it's my passion, my hobby. It's my family. It's my epicentre. Football has given me everything in life, beyond family. I don't really want to do much else. I could do it all the time, I love it that much. I'm very passionate about the game in all ways. And when I'm not doing it, I'm watching it.'

14

The Power of Partnership

THE FIRST name on the Her Game Too website partnership page is Fair Game UK. There is further tangible evidence of their connection, with Her Game Too founder Caz also being a policy advisor for them, specialising in helping to build a more inclusive and equal atmosphere in football. Both campaigns have shared values that reflect, resonate and amplify each other's strategies.

Led by the indefatigable CEO and AFC Wimbledon Trust board member Niall Couper, Fair Game UK has a clear focal point and catalyst. Supported by a growing list of ambassadors including Sky Sports' Hayley McQueen, the BBC's Dion Dublin and former Liverpool player John Scales, the drive for fairness and inclusivity chimes with Her Game Too, but Fair Game pursues the cause with a different strategy. One of the key drivers for them is to engage, enthuse and activate MPs to create and support legislation in pursuit of their aims.

The growing band of professional clubs working with Fair Game (31 at the last count) spans the Football League and non-league, and they are grouped regionally. There were some real seminal moments in the growth of partner clubs before the Everton 'big bang'. In late October 2021, not only did Montrose become the first Scottish club to join the

HGT partnership movement but Sheffield FC, considered the world's oldest club, also got on board. With each new club that commits to the principles of football for all, the Her Game Too manifesto becomes further embedded in the social fabric of football to the benefit of all fans.

HGT and Fair Game are similar, but not identical. Her Game Too focusses on awareness, education, research, community, content, club relationships, presence and campaigning, whilse Fair Game UK draws on the work done by MP Tracey Crouch, whose long-anticipated report into football has created a great deal of traction and profile for Fair Game. The group's mission statement starts with a quote from her:

> *'Football clubs are not ordinary businesses. They play a critical social, civic and cultural role in their local communities. They need to be protected – sometimes from their owners who are, after all, simply the current custodians of a community asset.'*

Tracey Crouch MP, 22 July 2021

***

Niall's opening salvo also resonates with the ethos of Her Game Too, appealing to the strong bonds we all have with our clubs to forge a better future for the game.

'Fair Game wants fans to be able to put on their club shirt, proud of everything it stands for and safe in the knowledge that the heritage and traditions of their club will always be there. Never before have clubs come together like this, but we know that now is the time. We have been working closely with over 30 world-renowned academics and experts to address the problems football faces. This document is the result of over six months of hard work. We want a different future. We need transparency. We need to incentivise good clubs.'

Her Game Too's mission statement approaches their task with a similar sense of determined focus:

'Here at Her Game Too, we see the value in everyone. We strive to be a catalyst for positive change, and we are driven by the same ideas we initially founded our Non-Profit Organisation upon: support, empowerment, and progress.

'Her Game Too was founded by 12 passionate female football fans, who are committed to growing the campaign to foster an ethos in football in which women are welcomed and respected equally.'

Four overlapping and overarching aspirations connect both campaigns and have shared set of values.

Open and Transparent

Like Her Game Too, Fair Game UK is determined to be open and transparent; for Her Game Too it is an explicit commitment to plough back any funds from merchandising and sponsorship in to the women's and girls' grassroots game development. Many of the messages for HGT are driven by the strong and compelling personalities of founders Caz May and Lucy Ford. Similarly, Niall Couper is a linchpin for open and transparent dialogue, not only with stakeholders of Fair Game but also with a wide network of politicians, journalists and academics. His key target is to pursue transparent business structures as identified by four points in Fair Game's recent survey:

1. 'Clubs and leagues must ensure that they are open and honest with the regulator.

2. In any change in control of the club, the new owner must provide a clear and transparent outline of the proposed ownership structure (i.e. where the money ultimately comes from to buy the club) in order to complete the purchase.

3. A clear organisational structure with well defined, transparent and consistent lines of responsibility.

4. We wish to see football governed with fairness, openness and transparency at its core; honouring the mantra that the game can be a force for good and putting clubs at the heart of the communities they serve.'

Collaborative and Engaging

In my role as representative for the southern Fair Game clubs, there was a palpable sense of collaboration between the clubs and within the organisation. Networks of collegiality and communication are built locally and feed into a web of like-minded clubs across the UK. In some ways, being volunteers also creates a free spirit of working toward a common goal that we could otherwise walk away from at any time if we felt isolated or demotivated. Tapping into networks of well-connected people across the UK gave us tremendous momentum, as did the ability to call on highly respected people. It was a real boost to our cause when Kevin Day, from the outstanding podcast *The Price of Football,* accepted my invitation to reflect on what football needs and how it has been brought to such a parlous place:

'We long for the day when there is no need for the Price of Football: the day when the money in English football is distributed fairly amongst 92 clubs, the day when fans can afford tickets again, the day when football grounds are treated the same way as listed buildings, the day when there are proper tests to prevent speculators and sharks from taking over cherished football clubs, the day when the government recognises the unique place that football has in its community – not just as a historical link to long-lost crafts and traditions but as a vibrant modern-day hub for the people around it; as we saw recently when so many clubs (and players) helped their community through Covid.'

For Her Game Too, there is a strong sense of team effort, not only because the key decision-makers started from a group of 12, but also due to an implicit understanding that through collaboration, communication and inspiration, the tsunami of neanderthal negativity they face can be held in check and, through the magic of synergy, held to account, rather than becoming just another can kicked down the road by male, pale and stale football custodians.

Guided By Experts

When releasing its manifesto on 10 September, 2021, Fair Game UK could call on 40 experts ranging from our Caz, lecturers, CEOs, writers and policy advisors. Each step forward is analysed and evaluated by a wide range of skills and moderated by highly informed voices in the game. Overarching initiatives are intrinsic to creating a fairer game in the wider interests of football. The group's integrity rests on the creation of innovative but practical and equitable solutions to the challenges facing a post- (and possibly pre-) European Franchise League environment.

The Her Game Too, manifesto is predicated on one clarion call: respect and value women in the game. With such a clarity of purpose, the real experts are the women on the committee and the legion of followers, supporters, players and fans who share common values. To collect important information to feed into future initiatives they have either commissioned their own research or joined with other groups like the Scottish Football Supporters Association in October 2021.

Community-Focussed and Inclusive

There is a shared spirit of community and inclusivity between both campaigns. After all, Her Game Too allowed a man to write this book! One of the tremendously effective ways of creating a sense of community for HGT has been to sponsor a range of football teams. This has not only increased engagement and awareness but also made players feel part of a movement both on and off the pitch. HGT is also explicitly inclusive of campaigns to support LGBTQ+ rights and uses its platforms to share a message of weaponised kindness.

Fair Game makes it very clear in its manifesto how important inclusivity and diversity are:

'Clubs and leagues should establish effective policies, procedures and methods of engagement to foster and promote an inclusive and diverse culture.' Sports psychologist Pippa Grange, writing in *Radical Football*, eloquently explained the importance of what she calls a 'radical harmony':

'Diversity isn't just a numbers game, or an effort at representation. It is a raging resistance to sameness and staleness, a desperately needed avoidance of the monocultures that always lead to impoverishment.'[11]

***

Her Game Too and Fair Game UK are two sides of the same coin. Passionate, disparate and committed, they represent a future for football that any right-minded fan would crave. It is easy to feel demoralised by the poor governance and financial recklessness on display each week in the top two leagues, but hope really is the last thing to die.

***

To find out more about the powerful partnerships forming with Her Game Too, I spoke to Jo Kinney, an FA registered intermediary and head of women's football at Ignite Soccer Agency. After half an hour in her company, I came away feeling that here was a professional, committed and maternal figure who was driven by the welfare of her clients rather

---

11 Fleming, S. *Radical Football Jürgen Griesbeck and the Story of Football for Good* pp. 374-375, (Pitch Publishing. Kindle Edition).

than some of the agent motives we often read about in the top end of the men's game. It was no surprise to hear that the company is now the official partner of Her Game Too. Here is some of our conversation from late 2021:

'Ignite has been around for about two years. I joined last July. I was taken on as a player consultant to liaise with potential players, existing players and to take the company forward by being the head of women's recruitment, so for me, it's been really quick learning supported by Tom Weston, who started the company. With the women's side, it's very much a personal agency, how we look after the players, all their needs to take the pressure off them. Everything off the pitch is taken care of so that they can focus on their game. We have a number of academy players who we are supporting to fulfil their dreams of becoming full-time professionals.

'You're not a shark, you're an agent. I'd like to think that there's someone taking care of my child and got their best interests at heart. So, I would never put a player into a club they don't want to go to. That's not what we're about. We're about supporting the player and giving them the best opportunity to say to the girls "when you look back in ten or 15 years, you can say hand on heart you gave it your all. You have had the most opportunities, you've played at the highest level, you've reached the pinnacle of your career and there are no regrets about the journey." That's where I get my satisfaction from: helping the girls on their journey.

'I do believe in speaking to the girls once a week in text messages before a game and after a game about how they got on and where they're at because mindset and wellbeing are just as important as the girls' technical ability. If they don't merge you're never going to get the complete player. And of course, there is now much more money in the women's game. A lot of the girls are not necessarily on megabucks, but across the board, a lot of the girls in the Championship now are being able to operate full-time or play full-time or they're going full-time as the clubs recognise if you're working [outside of football] eight to nine hours a day and then travelling at the weekend and training twice or three to four times a week you're not giving yourself the best opportunity to play your best football.

'I think there's a real change in the attitude of men's clubs. Look at Crystal Palace for instance. They've got the new academy set-up there. There are fantastic facilities which the women's team get to use first, which is amazing.

'I'd say with Her Game Too it's the ripple effect. It starts with sexism in football but then I do believe Women in Football as well really support women to be on boards, so the gates are being pushed open; but as I work in the public eye, the abuse I've taken from men that I don't know through social media just because I happen to be an agent and have an interest in football is terrible.

'I don't see why I can't do what other people do just because I happen to have been born female.'

Half Love is not Real Love

In football-mad Colombia the men's league attracts huge and passionate support but, in 2019 in the women's game, people felt marginalised and were facing the prospect of a cancelled season. This seemed like another dispiriting example of disrespect and decline. But not this time.

A campaign called Half Fans was unveiled, starting with the then Categoría Primera A men's champions, Atlético Junior, whose club crest was split into two parts. One half was worn on the men's shirts and the other half on the women's. This caused huge online outrage (imagine that). The campaign then really kicked into gear, challenging assumptions that the men's team was the only one worthy of fan support.

Every other Colombian team then joined the movement. The women's season started on 13 July, 2019 and finished on 30 September with the second leg of the finals. América de Cali won their first league title following a 3-2 win on aggregate against Independiente Medellín. Attendances at women's games that season skyrocketed by 633 per cent, with their league play-off attracting a stunning 55,000 fans. The league sponsors Águila came up with the campaign which revolutionised the game and finally woke fans up to the idea that you only fully support your club if you follow the men and women. Whether it was simply to maximise their beer sales doesn't matter. Their innovative and confrontational campaign supercharged the women's game and gave plenty of food for thought to the global game about how to show women the respect they deserve.

The Sky's the Limit

Chris Hull, former EFL director of communications, now its Respect campaign ambassador, knows a good thing when he sees it. And, when he met Caz and Lucy after inviting them to Wembley Stadium for England's World Cup qualifier against Hungary, he could see their great progress and immense potential. I spoke to him in late 2021 to get his perspective on the partnerships HGT is forging.

'I initially Met Caz and Lucy towards the start of the pandemic. I was doing some work for Sky Sports and I was down at "The Mem". I put a couple of bits and pieces out on social media and Caz and Lucy responded to me. These guys are very passionate Bristol Rovers fans and we started following each other. I could tell how insightful their thoughts were on not just Rovers but football in general. We exchanged several messages and then out of the blue I saw this incredible movement that they created: Her Game Too. I got in contact with them and said, "I think this is absolutely brilliant" and this was in the first few days.

'Now five months on, the whole thing has exploded to another level. Incredible. I just said if there's anything I can do I'd love to support it, so we've kept in touch and, because of the ambassadorial work I do with Nationwide and the FA's Respect campaign, I've been in contact with them recently because it aligns very well with the FA's campaign and the work that Nationwide is doing. After all, their work is all under the banner of mutual respect and I think that's what we're looking for across football. That is one of the things that Her Game Too are pushing towards: an inclusive football environment for everybody.

'Anybody that has met Caz and Lucy knows they're incredibly engaging and friendly people and I wanted to help them. A few weeks back I invited them to a forthcoming England game and I introduced them to several people within the industry and they sat and chatted with David James for a lot of the night as well. The thing I said to them at the time was, "I know you both know that what you're doing is good, but let me tell you it's even better than that. It's absolutely exceptional." I consider them to be pioneers.

'The work they're doing with Her Game Too this year, which has been one of the most challenging years for many people for many decades, is one of the highlights of the global footballing year.

'Everything is aligned perfectly. They've got a fantastic name, a fantastic brand. They've got fantastic principles and this applies to all the founders. Their hard work and their perseverance: their focus and commitment – but also, they're incredibly smart, polite, respectful and intelligent people. I think this movement that they've created has the potential to be as big as they want it to be. Although it's significant in this country at the moment, I think it's got the ability to have resonance in over 100 countries. What they're doing has captured a fantastic moment in time.

'I spoke to Kelly Smith and Rachel Yankey about this last month because I've been involved in supporting women's football for over 20 years. I said, "When I was involved with Nationwide and the England team 15 or 20 years ago, if somebody had told you that women's football would be where it is today, what would you have said?" They both said they'd have just laughed. They are incredulous at the speed in which women's football has taken hold and the broadcasting contracts which have just come into play in 2021 are a massive game-changer.'

Adding to this feeling of increased profile and resources for the women's game, in November 2021 CBS decided to air the Women's Super League until at least 2024, with 57 games a season being shown on Paramount+ and some of the highest-profile matches on the CBS Sports Network. The three-season deal is understood to be valued at £7m annually. Yet another shot in the arm for the women's game.

The perfect example of Chris Hull's description of Her Game Too as a fantastic name and brand came in October 2021. Gateshead FC and Nuffield Health Newcastle Hospital joined forces with HGT to launch Breast Cancer Awareness Month. In *Northern Insight*'s February 2022 edition, 'Raising Awareness of Women's Health Through the Power of Football', a Nuffield spokesperson shared how:

'At Nuffield Health Newcastle Hospital, we are committed to educating and advocating the importance of women's health at every stage of life. Through supporting Her Game Too, we hope to not only reinforce our stance that football should be a sport for all to enjoy, we also hope to raise awareness of women's health and its importance.'

Triangulating the fanbase and media reach of Gateshead FC, Her Game Too and Nuffield Hospital, they also ran a campaign highlighting awareness of cervical cancer in March 2022 that HGT co-founder Amy Clement wholeheartedly endorsed:

'It's great to have a well-known healthcare provider like Nuffield Health speaking out in support of our aim to make football safer for women and girls. At Her Game Too, we're working hard to create strong relationships with club trusts, sponsors and local communities to educate people on the importance of creating a welcoming environment for young girls and women. The more support we receive the sooner we can create a safer and more inclusive atmosphere for female fans today and for the next generation.'

And the partnerships just kept coming. On 12 January 2022, HGT announced that Select Soccer would now be the latest group in their exponentially-expanding stable. They provide coaching for boys and girls just across the estuary from me, in Torquay, focussing on enjoyment and safety over cut-throat competition. Players start from as young as four and, for the girls, an incredible 95 per cent of them are on a professional pathway. Not only are they an engine for change, but they invite equality, diversity and inclusion irrespective of ability, gender or age.

The following month saw the launch of a partnership with The World at Her Feet, whose mission statement, 'Empower to Aspire', drove a service to mentor, train and coach players, clubs and coaches, focussing on providing services affordable to everyone and with many of their offerings given for free. As they describe it:

'By offering players, coaches and clubs alike support, advice, information and training, we aim to give everybody a platform in which to improve themselves and take themselves further within the sport.'

These groups would only work with a trusted, respected brand to get their message across and they certainly chose the right people with Her Game Too.

15

Short Story: A Game of Two Halfwits

'GET YOUR tits out for the lads.'

Andy Gray's and Richard Keys's presenting colleague Clare Tomlinson was preparing herself to go live to camera at Cardiff's Millennium Stadium. The dinosaur duo were 'helpfully' wolf-whistling at her, and someone was filming them. This 30-second video would come back to haunt Gray and Keys in 2014 when it was leaked to Football Ramble: it was a strategic piece of timing that helped derail their planned return to the small screen.

Keys had already had the gall to describe his previous behaviour as a 'private bit of banter' and 'a light-hearted quip', while maintaining that 'dark forces' were behind him resigning from BSkyB in 2011. Qatar-based Al Jazeera and BeIn Sports have since had no qualms about paying the pair an annual king's ransom to present football for them, which feels like yet another reason why 2022's men's World Cup is in Qatar and the women's edition next year is in Australia and New Zealand. So why was Gray sacked from Sky, and why did Keys then resign?

It's 1811 – sorry 2011 – and, just before Bolton (remember when they were good?) played Chelsea (remember when they were skint?), anchors Keys and Gray are hauled off punditry duty for their offending women trying to create a profile in the game: from executives like Karren Brady to officials like Sian Massey. Victims of 'hot mics' (we have to assume that a furious female colleague 'accidentally' left the mics on) they shared chapter and verse on how creepily predatory their particular brand of 'banter' was for female colleagues forced to endure it. Keys later claimed they were the victims of a set-up in an interview with *The Athletic* in 2021 that marked a decade since 'Bantergate'. Talking to reporter Jack Pitt-Brooke in January 2021 Keys complained:

'Don't forget, neither of us were caught behind an open mic. What happened to me was recorded on a telephone in that studio; it seems to me it was done with a specific purpose.'[12]

This is an astonishing claim, when what they said is equally reprehensible to a single female colleague as well as millions of Sky viewers. In their Sky Sports kingdom, the prehistoric pair had started with the misogynist's default position of how, supposedly, women don't understand the offside rule – directing that criticism at assistant referee Sian Massey. (Fast forward a decade and VAR has made 'women' of us all. If you understand someone explaining the ever-changing rules then you are not listening properly.)

Karren Brady has her faults, as West Ham fans will tell you, but Keys's acidic review of her newspaper column was purely based on her gender, not her agenda, in an age of ghost-written agent spin passing itself off as journalism:

'The game's gone mad. See charming Karren Brady this morning complaining about sexism? Yeah. Do me a favour, love.'

---

12 *The Athletic*. 'Keys and Gray. Somebody's f***ed up big': Ten years on from Keys and Gray at Sky Sports, 24 January 2021, https://theathletic.co.uk/2332184/2021/01/24/sky-sports-sian-massey-ellis-richard-keys-andy-gray/?redirected=1. Accessed 1st October 2021.

It's important to note that Keys at least had the decency to call Massey and apologise, but they always invoke the banter defence – saying it's all part of the rough and tumble in and around the game. Massey was to derail the banter bus here too. Rather than get defensive, she simply told Keys that he should have known better. One nil …

Just when you thought the bottom of the barrel had been scraped, Keys spotted a marketing opportunity in 2019, selling greetings messages on cameo.com. Alongside Mister T (for £300 a time!), Nick Hexum (nor me) and Kenny G (where did all the money go Kenny?) Keys saw his gap in the market. His hook on the site read:

'Let's "smash it" together and have a bit of banter.'

According to his bio on the site, 'Richard Keys is currently not taking any bookings at this moment,' which must be devastating news to his loyal army of seven site fans.

Andy Gray is actually 'smashing it' relative to Keys. Charging £53 a throw or £368 for corporate clips (wow) he sensibly positions himself as a 'former pro soccer player' and his 95 mostly positive reviews focus on his legendary playing days for Villa and Everton.

While Gray was to come out of the sorry mess with some semblance of dignity through not deciding to keep digging the hole he was in, Keys jumped in the JCB and kept excavating.

Gray was sacked by Sky in January 2011 after a video emerged during a rehearsal for a Christmas special inviting colleague Charlotte Jackson, 'Charlotte just tuck that in for me, love.'

Keys could have held out if not for more damning video evidence coming to light from a discussion with fledgling presenter Jamie Redknapp. Putting his feet up on the glass studio table he lasciviously shares what he thought the former Liverpool man would do if he was anywhere near his former girlfriend. Sky scuttled to film a 'mia culpa' with

Keys. The only problem was that Keys was in no mood to apologise unreservedly. While he did, during the hour-and-a-half interview admit to 'prehistoric banter' and detailed his apology to Massey ('she and I enjoyed some banter together') it was the 'dark forces' wot done it, not him. But he knew which way this tide was turning and decided to jump just before he was pushed out. However, even a decade later, Keys retains the victim's stance. His revisionist defence in his 2021 interview with Pitt-Brooke was how 'it was a set-up, of course it was. But they made capital out of it.'[13]

But we have one thing to thank the pair for. They were the watershed moment that has ushered in a far more inclusive culture in which a range of voices now analyses games irrespective of their chromosomes or skin pigmentation. But I can't help thinking that somewhere in Qatar, a hairy-handed man is putting together a His Game Too campaign. Frightening. Even for Richard Keys who, by April 2021 seemed to have had some sort of epiphany when describing the performance of trailblazing official Rebecca Welch:

'And great work Rebecca Welch. Please hurry up and save us from the mediocrity that we suffer week after week in the PL.'

Key's newfound dream moved one step closer to realisation on 8 January 2022 when Welch became the first woman to referee an FA Cup third-round tie. The following day Rwandan Salima Mukansanga became the first woman to officiate at an African Cup of Nations match, which must have made him even more excited.

Maybe there is hope, after all …

---

13 *The Athletic*. 'Keys and Gray. Somebody's f***ed up big': Ten years on from Keys and Gray at Sky Sports, 24 January 2021, https://theathletic. co.uk/2332184/2021/01/24/sky-sports-sian-massey-ellis-richard-keys-andy-gray/?redirected=1. Accessed 1st October 2021.

16.

The Power of Purpose

MY PREVIOUS conversations with Her Game Too director, former managing director of Oldham Athletic and now CEO of FC United of Manchester, Natalie Atkinson, inspired me to reflect on the role clubs play in being an engine for change in their local community.

Natalie wrote the following:

'From Football Club to Football Hub

'Described by the Cambridge Dictionary as "the central part of something where there is most activity", a hub defines exactly what a football club should be: a catalyst for a community that provides much more than 90 minutes of football, a community hub that spreads spokes of engagement through the lives of its locals by proactive initiatives that broadcast the very best of community, culture and society. Female representation within a club is key to showcasing diversity but more importantly confirming that football should be equal on and off the field. 'Diversity of thought is crucial in any environment. Women think differently to men: we empathise differently, we work and act differently to men, which offers a complementary way of delivering a vision. The more diverse your club is from boardroom to ball-girl, the better it functions.

'A club has a purpose: whether that be the 90 match-minutes, delivering a business strategy, securing funding to create a community training facility, a walking football programme or a disability initiative for a local school. The variety should represent the vision of the town, its culture, and the club.

'Stakeholders are crucial in delivering a football hub's purpose: who they are, their function, their contribution, and how they support delivering the plan and vision. A stakeholder can be a local school, business, or person. The key driver is for them to be local to a club hub that shares their core values.

'Female ambassadors within the hub are also key. I know Caz has spoken about this with HGT in terms of having a fan as an ambassador to raise awareness that females are welcome, it's safe and that it should be equal on the terraces. Coupled with this, the football hub should be running an extensive range of female-led programmes: be that girl's and women's teams, matches sharing the stadia pitch or raising awareness of International Women's Day. At Southport FC we showcased a female within the club each day of the week of International Women's Day to highlight the women within the club, the roles they played and how important women are to the club as a hub.'

***

Writing in *Radical Football Jürgen Griesbeck and the Story of Football for Good*, Brentford's only south Asian non-executive director and long-time member of Football For Good, Preeti Shetty, laid out the five steps she feels allow purpose to thrive and make a difference because, for her, football as, 'the most viewed sport in the world, is one of the most important battlegrounds for purpose'.

For her, purpose, 'needs to come from an innate sense of community or identity. It needs to come from looking within and understanding why you are here, understanding the role you play in your community or with your fans, the value you are adding by what you do.'

For Shetty, knowing your purpose is the first step and immediately challenging yourself about what the next step needs to be and how it will be measured using tangible metrics, is the follow-up action. Step three is summarised by the Superman quote, 'with great power comes great responsibility' and step four is the point where we challenge ourselves to recognise what success looks like. For Shetty, purpose is shaped by data driving into the fifth step that sees any failure to be forward looking as a step back.

It's understandable to feel demoralised by tranches of patronising, misogynistic attitudes to women in sport, but there are opportunities to drive a front-foot female agenda as a confident, considered, and loyal customer base. Released on 5 October 2021 by the sports marketing agency The Space Between, a wide-ranging survey of how attitudes and behaviours differ between male and female sports fans gave a real insight into maximising the 'considerable value on the table' of women in sport. Interviews with 500 sports fans over the age of 16 aimed to evaluate differences in attitude and engagement towards women's sport.

The survey started by acknowledging the strides already made in women's sport from, 'being undersold and underutilised to becoming an opportunity that brands are increasingly waking up to'. The tone of the report resonates with Amazon founder Jeff Bezos's Day One philosophy. His credo, even with $171.9 (don't forget the .9) billion in the bank as of 26 April 2022 (according to Forbes Real Time Rich List) is to think and act as if you are a perpetual start-up. So embedded is this thought process in Bezos's mind that his office is in the Day One Building.

The pioneering power of communal purpose identified in women's sport has a vitality and traction long beaten out of many men's sports by decades of complacent patriarchy. One key driver identified in the report was how the Covid 19 pandemic created a surge in online engagement, a platform considered by women to be a key arena for engaging with brands who support women's sport. The survey found that women are often quicker adopters of tech than men, something the authors feel has been largely ignored by brands and rights holders. It appears that too much of the attention is focussed on quantity in the men's fan game versus the quality of purpose in women's sport where fans, both male and female, will tend to be early adopters of technology (74 per cent of the women respondents liked to keep up to date with the latest tech compared to 44 per cent of men's sports fans).

This perceived disparity between men's and women's sport is partly driven by a similar imbalance in the amount of media coverage that furthers the quote by children's rights campaigner Marian Wright Edelman:

'You can't be what you can't see.'

***

As the survey highlights:

'Our respondents are fully supportive of more coverage to close the "visibility gap", with 81 per cent of women's sports fans agreeing that it should be covered in the same way as men's sport, with 46 per cent strongly in agreement.'

As described by Keith Kropman, the chief marketing officer of Vitality, sponsorship can be an effective way to close the 'gender play gap'. This media coverage imbalance creates a vicious cycle where less attention creates less profile that leads back to less attention. But it is easy to overlook the fact that men make up 41 per cent of the crowds watching women's professional sport. This is driven partly by how the Premier League is a largely non-competitive environment. The champions will come from the quartet of Chelsea, Liverpool and the two Manchester clubs. In the 2021/2 season, the three relegated clubs were highly likely to be Norwich, Burnley and Watford (even typing this with a dozen games to go). The other dozen teams are scrapping for lower-level European competition and prize money for league places. The WSL may be topped by the triumvirate of London powerhouses in Chelsea, Tottenham and Arsenal, but The Space Between survey indicates that women's football provides a richer experience than simply points on the board. Fostering an environment that is 'inclusive, inspiring and welcoming' is highly appetising to brands. It also means that fans are not looking to copy and paste experiences with the men's game but enjoy each environment using different criteria. As a season-ticket holder for both Exeter City's men's and women's teams, the experience of watching matches is markedly different. For the men, it is about points or bust in a more binary environment. But at Exeter City Women it is more about a celebration of shared core values by people wanting to engage, connect and respect their fellow fans, irrespective of the colour on their scarves. Speeds Meadow Cullompton becomes a catalyst for fans to share flags, food and friendship. The survey suggested that women fans are, '21 per cent more likely to believe they have a strong connection with other fans of the same sport than men's sports fans (71 per cent versus 50 per cent) which indicates a genuinely differentiated sense of community within women's sport.'

This sense of community is furthered by the way women athletes were viewed in the survey. Women, by a 23 per cent margin, were seen as role models in the women's game compared to the men's. A tremendously successful opportunity to illustrate this came in 2021's The Hundred cricket tournament where men and women shared equal billing and often the same venues on the same days, which gave the female players a huge level of visibility and credence that has helped to inspire others and evolve into defining the tournament through sport and not gender. Combined with a more tech-savvy orientation, 80 per cent of women agree that the power brands can attach to women's sport is vital in growing profile and momentum. The 'halo effect', where the strongest attributes of a brand and sport are placed together in the hope that the best aspects of each will rub off on the other, creates a currency of validation and legitimisation that should benefit both halves of the halo. Indeed, as the survey points out, '76 per cent of women's sport fans agree that they notice brands when watching sports events and 74 per cent agree that they notice brands using sports in their advertising, compared to 44 per cent and 57 per cent of men's sport fans respectively'.

Women's stronger recognition of brands in sport is also actioned more stridently than their male counterparts. Sixty-eight per cent of the women surveyed feel they are likely to consider the brand seen at a sports venue compared to only 44 per cent for men. The gap is even wider when it comes to using word of mouth to spread brand awareness, where 64 per cent of women say they have talked about brands they have seen at sports compared to only 37 per cent of men. This leads to one of the real headline findings in the survey:

'Women's sports fans are 25 per cent more likely to purchase the brand sponsor of their favourite sport than men's sports fans.'

Sport branding has become a mature arena where most marketing gains are marginal. To uncover a market with a potential upside of a quarter should get advertisers salivating at the prospects it invites. Of course, these are intentions to buy rather than actions but suggest motive (or lack of it for men) to act on the purchase impulse as a way of rewarding those placing their brand next to women's sports.

Another key area highlighted in the survey is how much women fans tend to be driven by a more progressive and purposeful attitude that sees their sports as an arena to bring about societal change, especially focussing on gender equality but also environmental concerns, social justice and ethical practices. But, for brands, it isn't only an exercise in plastering their logo over women's sports to maximise their return on investment. Women sports fans often hold brands up to a higher standard than men, according to the survey. Brands in women's sports are required to address important societal issues, with 50 per cent of the female respondents strongly agreeing with this approach. In contrast, only 20 per cent of male respondents felt the same. This attitude by the female respondents serves as a self-filtering system for brands. If they don't satisfy their specific criteria, then they won't be welcome. For brands that can satisfy these expectations, there is a great opportunity to create loyalty and activation. This is supported by the finding that:

'Women's fans are twice as likely to be values-driven when choosing one brand over another, with 40 per cent deeming it very important that brands "reflect my values", versus 20 per cent among men's sports fans.'

The Space Between survey indicates an incredibly exciting tipping point is approaching in women's sports. With an authentic story to tell, high levels of activation by extremely committed, collegial and motivated followers, women's sports provide a highly dynamic landscape in which to place brands that can provide mutual benefit for both the sponsors and the sponsored. Above all, women's sports have now become an arena to show the intoxicating momentum created by playing and supporting sports that unleash the power of purpose. Count me in.

Through Crisis Comes Opportunity

The joint report 'Women's Sport: Bouncing Back from the Pandemic?' published in October 2021 by Leaders in Sport and Sky Sports suggested that the Covid-19 pandemic and year and a half of lockdowns have given sports fans a chance to reset and refresh their attitudes about the sports they follow. For women's football, it suggests that the values-driven and communally purposeful approach often found in women's sport and draining out of men's has created a strong appetite to support them.

The headline rates make inspiring reading, not only for those involved with women's sports but also the brands and corporations evaluating whether to move away from a men's game dominated by gambling companies and welcoming with open arms human rights violators and state-sponsored misogynists. Twenty-one per cent of UK adults have increased their following of women's sports since March 2020 and the Women's Super League is considered to be in the vanguard of increasing visibility for all women's sports. Much of this can be put down to the increased profile created by the WSL's £8m Sky Sports deal, coming soon after the hybrid coverage of The Hundred in cricket, where viewers could watch selected games on terrestrial screens as well as behind a paywall. Respondents also highlighted how it was not only the quantity of coverage but the production values invested in it that helped heighten their experiences.

The report amplifies some of the findings from sports marketing agency The Space Between. It was released the previous week and it also suggested that men make up a significant and growing audience for the women's game. This is likely to be caused by the push factors of being weary about top-level men's football now often being the plaything of state-sponsored sports-washing fronts, clubs diverting funds through their official George Town in the Cayman Islands headquarters rather than rainy Manchester M16 and the lack of any real title jeopardy in an English Premier League season's outcomes. But, increasingly, there are significant pull factors of a women's game across a range of sports that are not only surviving but thriving. The 24 per cent increase in men watching women's sports represents the biggest area of increase in the survey. The hybrid broadcast model that worked so successfully in cricket's The Hundred has also been a strong pull factor in attracting more of a mass audience, with one game in each WSL round being shown on the BBC and the FA Player, a platform that is not only professionally designed but supported by a strong social media presence that feeds into the Barclays FA Women's Super League Twitter feed of 200,000 followers and an Instagram following of 228,000.

One of the most significant findings for the future of women's sports coverage was how 41 per cent of respondents feel both the men's and women's games should be given equal profiles. To drive this parity, almost half of respondents believe that sports advertising should select a similar number of male and female athletes in their campaigns as a third of people asked feel they have developed their awareness of the games through viewing and interacting with the stars promoting them through advertising and social media.

Released in July 2021, Deloitte's Annual Review of Football mentioned Covid an astonishing 113 times. But, for all of football's ongoing challenges, there are beacons of hope for the women's game. Deloitte's report headline was:

'In 2019/20, the stakeholders in women's football took action to reduce the barriers to entry, striving to increase professionalisation, provide viable opportunities for participation and improve player welfare across the globe.'

Reviewing the 2019/20 season Deloitte highlighted the increasing levels of commercial investment in the women's game that leveraged the heightened global profile of women's football turbocharged by the 2019 Women's World Cup in France. A key domestic driver was Barclays' reported £10m, three-year sponsorship of the Women's Super League. This helped develop the product and Sky combined with the BBC to provide the platform for a reported £8m for the 2021/22 season. But, as the survey points out, there were more positives than just the welcome injection of more commercial capital:

'Commercial partnerships not only deliver cash but also drive increased exposure through greater activation opportunities. We expect this increased funding to also feed into greater professionalism in many areas including improved regulation, governance and welfare standards.'

Even the country that doesn't own Newcastle United showed a measure of enlightenment when the 'Saudi Arabian Football Federation (SAFF) launched its first women's league, the Women's Community Football League.'

These initiatives and prudent decisions led the report's authors to project a positive future for the women's game:

'The profile of women's football continues to grow at pace. Recent seasons have seen elite clubs incorporate and invest in their women's teams. As noted in our 2021 edition of the Deloitte Football Money League, 18 of the top 20 revenue-generating clubs in world football now have a women's team.'

By the end of April 2022, this new economic reality was emerging where businesses increasingly identified women's football as a fertile and lucrative arena for returns on investment. A heartening example was when social soccer scouting app Gloria Football paid €10m for a three-year deal to be title sponsors of Spain's first professional women's football league. Founder and CEO Victoire Cogevina described the investment as 'purely business-driven'. Another intriguing facet of the sponsor's approach is its determination to create marketing exclusively tailored to women. Launching the partnership, Cogevina told the press:

'I'm a big believer that this asset, which is women's football, is at the very beginning of its growth. I'm pretty sure that in a couple of years from now, there is a big chance that Spain will become the leading women's league in Europe – if not the world – and that €10 million will seem like a very small price.'

Viewing women's football as a start-up is an interesting perspective, harking back to the Bezos Day One philosophy. But rather than seeing the project as underdeveloped, Cogevina sees the women's game as more dynamic, nimble and with more opportunities for growth and lucrative investments than the men's game. This new financial landscape for European football was clarified at the end of April 2022 when the Women's Serie A announced that for the 2022/3 season, it would turn fully professional for the first time. The 12-team league was headlined in the 2021/2 season by Juventus, Roma and Inter Milan and AC Milan but also included lesser-known teams like Sassuolo and Pomigliano. So now, for 2022/3, women's European leagues in France, Germany, Spain and Italy will provide players with career pathways across a network of countries that continue to raise the bar for the women's game, while the Women's Super League in England can call on five fully professional years and counting to show, share and spotlight developmental challenges for their sister leagues across the channel.

Even the Football Money League itself commits to, 'developing the Money League, and our insights and publications more widely, to report more fully on the women's game in future'.

The growing stature of women's football presents a significant opportunity for clubs to increase brand profile and grow revenue, while also achieving on-pitch success. The exponential growth in the women's game was underscored in June 2021 when FIFA conducted its first-ever 'comprehensive analysis of the elite women's football landscape'. Processing results from 30 leagues and almost 300 clubs focussing on 'sporting, governance, finance, fan engagement and player-related topics that look to enhance the move to increasing professionalism in the women's game', I picked out nine key findings that suggest a positive and building momentum:

1. For a women's club to achieve significant growth, it is important to be a standalone organisation rather than an affiliate. The report found that independent women's teams generate 110 per cent of the average club revenue in their league compared with 98 per cent for affiliate clubs.

2. Carefully curating a pipeline of age and development teams helps improve national team ranking. If a league has 80 per cent or more clubs developing these pipelines the average national-team ranking is 13, compared to a ranking of 28 for all other leagues.

3. The team with access to the most facilities, on average, achieved a higher league position in the last five years: 50 per cent of teams with access to the most facilities per league won the league in the last five years, compared with only 23 per cent for all other clubs.

4. In 65 per cent of leagues, teams with coaches who had a higher-tier licence outperformed teams whose head coaches had a lower-tier licence.

5. Commercial independence: revenue is higher for clubs that negotiate sponsorship contracts for the women's team only, with 72 per cent of clubs reporting that they negotiate some of their sponsorship contracts just for the women's team.

6. Sponsorship revenue is a key differentiator for both clubs and leagues. The clubs that generate the highest revenue (over \$1m) raise over half (53 per cent) of it through sponsorship, compared to less than a third (29 per cent) for clubs averaging revenue of less than \$1m.

7. Broadcast rights represent a significant growth opportunity for the women's game. Broadcast income, on average, accounts for only six per cent of club revenue and 18 per cent of league revenue, a wide departure from its importance to the men's game. Increasing the proportion of matches produced and subsequently broadcast could

increase the appeal of the women's game to broadcasters. Broadcasting matches is not only a source of revenue, it also significantly contributes to increasing the exposure of the women's game.

8. Player power: having a collective voice that speaks on behalf of the players can be a powerful tool to help improve player conditions and welfare. Of the leagues with a players' association or union, 63 per cent have a minimum player wage, compared with only 17 per cent that do not have player representation.

9. Sponsorship revenue is linked to social media followings. This was highlighted in late October 2021 when American NWSL expansion club Angel City FC announced that one per cent of all ticket sales would be given to players who activated their social media account to attract more fans. Despite not having kicked a ball yet, the club sold 11,000 season tickets in 72 hours and by their first game on 19 March this had risen by another 3,000, to the envy of men's clubs globally. The 'Fan Fuelled Player fund' could net each player several thousand dollars a year and shows an innovative approach to activating players as promoters of the games and club in the community and globally.

***

Every report that comes out builds on a sense that a tipping point in women's sport has been reached. Supported by previous pay parity between both genders, such as September 2021's decision by the US Soccer Federation to offer identical contracts to both the men's and women's teams, an ecosystem is evolving to drive unstoppable momentum towards parity. Better late than never.

17

Short Story: Bringing Out the Best in Men

TALKING TO *The Athletic*'s Jay Harris in September 2021, self-confessed wild child and man still coming to terms with being the son of George, Calum Best spoke openly and honestly about how diving headlong into the job of chairman at Dorking Wanderers Ladies FC has done far more for him than he can ever do for them. Still only 41, he has packed in decades of partying and various TV adventures prefaced by the word '*Celebrity*': *Love Island*, *Go Dating* and *Big Brother* amongst many others.

There have been toe-curling lows, like being a contestant in Daytime TV shonky fodder *Come Dine With Me* in 2010, but also a project to be proud of as narrator of BT's sumptuous documentary *True Genius* on 26 May 2021 – a worthy legacy piece commemorating his mercurial dad. Best knows he is at a crossroads where, despite wealth and a level of fame, he needs to use his heritage and skills to create something with far more heft and permanence than a score out of ten for someone's chicken vindaloo on a daytime TV show. He shared with *The Athletic*:

'Although people won't know me for football, I have a heritage that is football and I've never figured out what I could do with that.'

This brings us to Best's arrival at the sixth tier of women's football. The Her Game Too movement was the catalyst for him to reassess where his life was going and how he wanted to change his personal story's arc. Indeed, when interviewed for *The Athletic*, he was proudly wearing an HGT hoodie and animatedly related how the Dorking first-team squad now warm-up before matches in Her Game Too T-shirts. As he shared with Jay Harris:

'I saw a campaign called Her Game Too. I looked at it and it was a group of ladies who made a video about the sexist abuse they got at games, and I was triggered by it. It sucks that they feel that way and that wherever they go to watch the game that's happening. It shouldn't be that way; no one should be uncomfortable to go to a game.'[14]

Coupled with watching the video, in which members of Her Game Too exchange sexist comments on pieces of paper while wearing their beloved team shirts and which has now clocked up two million views, Best felt a call to arms and a chance to find a cause that traded on his passion and ideas rather than simply his surname. He had previously spent much of his young life trying to stand up for his dad's spiralling descent into alcoholism cruelly exposed across the television world in 1990's *Wogan* show, where the clearly inebriated star stumbled through an agonising and embarrassing exchange. Now Calum has something meaningful to stand up for. As the Dorking Ladies' director of football Kat Browne related to Harris:

'I work full-time in football and face sexism frequently. It's always been there in terms of things that we have to overcome as female coaches and players within the game.

14 *The Athletic*. 'Meet Dorking Ladies chairman ... Calum Best: 'I want to take us to play dad's old team.' 16 September 2021, https://theathletic.com/2823576/2021/09/16/meet-dorking-ladies-chairman-calum-best-i-want-to-take-us-to-play-dads-old-team/?article_source=search&search_query=calum%20best. Accessed 16 September 2021.

Calum came in and said that this campaign was close to his heart and he wanted to do more. We want to raise that awareness, so we got that partnership with them.'

Best can see that, the more he gives to Dorking, the more he will receive in return and it surprises, even shocks him how much he is being nourished through a project stripped back to the absolute basics of previous attendances averaging 30 (now doubled after he underwrote tickets for the rest of last season) and the players scratching around for somewhere to train (until he secured the club's Meadowbank Stadium twice a week). It has disarmed and surprised a man used to trading off or fighting against the family name. Something has chimed with his personality and stage in life that this is a real battle worth fighting for instead of parading budgie smugglers on a tropical beach. There is even a feeling of shock in how energised he is with this project:

'I can't believe how fully involved I am,' he says. 'It's not just about being a chairman of a club and creating some commercial deals, it's about being fully invested and letting the players know I'm supporting them.'

His aim for Dorking to be playing Manchester United in the league may seem fanciful, but stranger things have happened. Whatever he achieves in this Surrey town, Calum has the chance to challenge himself and learn how to succeed through grind, not glamour. Listening to *Soccer AM* in mid-January 2022 it was also clear that this, unlike some of his earlier projects, is not a passing fad. He told the show's huge audience and one million Twitter followers how his role has, 'gone from strength to strength. I absolutely love it.' This was made clear when, after being awarded the monthly Her Game Too award for January 2022, his face reflected absolute joy at the decision. It won't be easy for someone used to living in a gilded cage, but if he can break out of it, he has a chance to build meaningful achievements that can stand as his true legacy.

18

The Power of Opportunity

AMY CANAVAN'S thoughtful and thought-provoking documentary in January 2022 raised some uncomfortable questions about women's treatment in football but sees hope that the tide is slowly turning to a point where a journalist will be judged on their performance rather than their chromosome count.

Setting the scene, sportswriter for *The Scotsman*, *Scotland on Sunday* and the *Edinburgh Evening News* Moira Gordon described the atmosphere when a woman would walk into the male-dominated world of a press box early in her career:

'It was like one of those horror movies the first time you walked down, where the door creaks and everybody stops and stares at you.'

Ginny Clark, the first and only female sports editor in Scotland 'was a zoo exhibit; there's no doubt about it' while for presenter Eilidh Barbour, when male commentators make mistakes it fuels light banter, but when a woman makes an error, 'it's not a mistake, it's that you don't know what you're talking about'.

This is supported by reporter Heather Dewar:

'It's almost like sometimes people are just waiting to pounce on the slightest mistake and that's purely because you're a female and because a lot of men out there don't think that females should be doing football reporting.'

Journalist and editor Kevin McKenna gives a blunt assessment of why so few men have shown women the respect they deserve. 'Male journalists are lazy; male newspaper executives who make these appointments are just lazy. They don't go the extra mile to see what's out there and they take what they think is the safe option.'

But there is hope. Building and broadening stories of inclusion and diversity are starting to percolate through the game at all levels from Everton's HGT partnership, Lewes FC's community ownership model and the rising profile of the WSL. As Jane Lewis eloquently explains:

'They're doing that knowing that they might get criticised for it, but they're sticking with that because they know the bigger picture is the more diverse you are the more engagement you're going to have with an audience and it's just the right thing to do.'

Eilidh Barbour is 'a big believer in you don't want to be what you can't see, so if you don't have a female commentator how does anybody know that you can be a female commentator?'.

Canavan concludes with the growing sense that better days are ahead for women in the beautiful game, a view shared by Graham Spiers, four-time winner of Scotland's Sports Journalist of the Year award:

'I think new generations of kids and journalists and young people have emerged who just have a more decent outlook: they just have a more modern outlook.'

This was a view resoundingly supported in February 2022 when a report by the Women's Sport Trust of 2021 on viewing figures for women's sport highlighted that, in the WSL and women's Hundred, 11 million new viewers were activated. Visibility Uncovered also noted that, as eye-catching as this headline figure was, it also came at a time when audiences for

TV watching in general were falling – and the good news kept coming. The report discovered that 5.9 million new viewers for the WSL had not watched any other sport in 2021 before the start of the season. These two headline events were also effective gateway experiences for fans to watch other women's sports as, according to the report, almost three-quarters of the five million new viewers for the women's Hundred then went on to watch other women's sports. And these figures were no flash in the pan. According to a BBC survey published in February 2022, they were part of an enduring trend. In 2017, the two sports (women's cricket and football) attracted 25.1 million pairs of eyes, which would increase by seven million by 2019 then, despite a Covid-induced dip in 2020, hit just shy of 33 million by 2021. This is an incredibly vibrant and relatively new market that enjoys an exponential rise no longer seen in the men's game. The case for EDI (equality, diversity and inclusion) as an economic opportunity was also eloquently put by a report released on 8 March 2022. Called the Commercial Case for Gender Equality it was driven by a quote from Tracey Crouch's Fan-Led Review:

'EDI should form a strong pillar of good corporate governance. It should be seen as a central part of any organisation's business plan and not an "add-on".'

The eight authors from academia and sports law focussed on eight key areas including boards, broadcasting and visibility, marketing and sponsorship and community and merchandise. Some areas show a frustrating lack of progress, like broadcasting, where it was found that only 11 per cent of participants were female, but in other areas like sponsorship, the huge growth that has not been seen in the men's game for years is a highly productive wave for future players, clubs, staff and businesses to ride. The 22-page, 6,000-word report showed that, with clear focus and agreed targets, women's football can continue to surge and, as the men's game continues to flirt with the highly damaging and divisive European Super League in all its guises, there is a phenomenal opportunity for even more market growth as fans question whether they want our beautiful game to go the fractured way of boxing with its myriad of 'World Champions' and competing governing bodies.

The ever readable and gloriously grumpy John Nicholson summarised the findings with his usual brutal logic writing in Football365.com on 17 February 2022:

'While no one is pretending these averages are incredibly high figures, for a sport coming from a very low base, for a sport that continues to be under-funded, for a sport that is fighting institutionalised bigotry, fighting denigration, fighting being made to feel worthless from a young age, and fighting being culturally excluded on the basis that playing sport is somehow not feminine, these are bloody good. The WSL and other sports are attracting, educating and building followers on a week-to-week basis in a way that men's football absolutely does not have to. And it's working.'

The momentum of blending women's teams into the daily lives of clubs is also increasing exponentially. Exeter City have welcomed Her Game Too and created set-piece games, weekends and consistent profile for the women's team through their legendary media team, and fully integrated the women's side of the club into the official website. There remains the frustrating issue of the women's 'home' games being a 30-minute drive from the stadium, but there is a will to keep the whole club together and find solutions to benefit everyone.

These are the kind of initiatives that will create meaningful traction and positive change, but there remain frustrating slights and oversights. Writing in *The Athletic* on 23 January 2022, Caoimhe O'Neill highlighted how Liverpool's men and women being scheduled side by side robbed the women's team of more fans and profile as they continued their march to the WSL as champions in the

2021/2022 season. The women attracted just under 900 fans, but surely some of the 52,824 at the men's game would have been open to supporting their female players, given the opportunity. Despite this kick-off clash, the crowd was only slightly below their average, so there is clearly a strongly loyal female football fan base to build on.

'Understandably a lot of fans feel the same frustration,' Jo Goodall, founder of Liverpool Women's Supporters Club, told *The Athletic*. 'We all want to be able to support and, where possible, watch both teams play. Some of our women's team's fans are season ticket holders for the men and it's really sad that they have to choose between the two games, with the men's games usually taking precedence due to the cost of season tickets.'

This is one more unintended consequence of the TV tail wagging the football dog. When they cherry-pick men's matches for maximum viewership, it cascades down to the women's fixtures and they will often have to accept whatever is imposed on them while the big money does the loudest talking. To be fair to Sky, they make their choices six weeks ahead of the fixture, but advanced train tickets, planning time off work and possibly booking hotels has a stronger financial imperative in the women's game, where resources are often tight (especially in the Championship). As O'Neill rightly identifies, a more holistic approach would have given fans a chance to support both teams and offered more oxygen of opportunity to help the women's game grow.

***

A campaign that showcased the power of opportunity was Women in Football's #GetOnside. It collected over 130 action pledges since its launch in September 2021, and its key aims were to provide more, 'opportunities for girls to play in school, celebrating the work already done by women in the football industry, and supporting the career progression of others in roles both on and off the pitch'.

The meaningful range of pledgers created a tremendous profile for the campaign. Joining Barclays were Aston Villa, Brighton, Everton, ITV Sport and the Scottish FA among many others with tangible and creative offers:

'We pledge to #GetOnside by doubling participation, fanbase and investment in women and girls' football in Wales,' said the Football Association of Wales.

'We pledge to #GetOnside by becoming a Women in Football corporate member, to enable us to support our people with the best leadership, training and development we can,' said Sky Sports.

'We pledge to #GetOnside by making Hampden Park the new home of the Scottish Women's National Team,' said the Scottish FA.

'We pledge to #GetOnside by offering paid internships to two women – one at Villa Park and one at our Bodymoor Heath training centre, said Aston Villa FC.

Villa took a step further at the end of January 2022 by producing a video to, 'shine a light on the amazing women currently working at the club and Aston Villa Foundation'. The first video focussed on Bodymoor Heath finance and recruitment worker Angela Lewis and under-16s and under-21s head coach in the Regional Talent Club Kerri Welsh. Creating a narrative and backstory for women that thrive in such a wide range of roles in football shows girls aspiring to do the same that, whatever their skills, there is a role for them in the game and the pathways are already being cut, established and amplified by capable and hard-working women. Villa's support of this process is unequivocal:

'Aston Villa Football Club welcomes and encourages women from all backgrounds to join our team both on and off the pitch.'

Men's teams are also helping women to get onside. Beth Lumsden combines a busy full-time job as an estate agent with being a striker for Oxford United Women. Her story of long journeys, personal sacrifice and feverish time-management is typical of many women making their way in the game. But when she is not banging in goals for the National League South side, she is part of the men's training sessions. After a chance conversation with coach Karl Robinson, Lumsden was welcomed into training when she explained to him how she felt short-changed for contact time in training, which is not surprising given all the restrictions on female players in this tier-three league who are yet to use these skills to pay the bills.

Her experiences in the men's sessions have been, as she related to *The Athletic* reporter Nancy Frostick in late November 2021, wholly positive. Despite having to commit to a 120-mile round trip to training, Lumsden feels stronger and sharper for the experience. The benefits of these intense, high-tempo sessions have not only been felt physically for her. She told Frostick:

'In the training sessions, everything is a lot quicker. From session to session, everything is a faster tempo. When I'm in the sessions it's not so much about physically matching them but mentally matching them.'

***

Two identical Spanish fixtures were the perfect case study of how attitudes to integrity and tradition can create opportunities or damage reputations. For the men, their Spanish Super Cup not only changed its place in the calendar but was shipped out en masse to Saudi Arabia, as Barcelona coach Ernesto Valverde candidly admitted, purely for the money. The Saudis also meddled with the traditional format to include the two top teams in La Liga and the finalists in the Copa del Rey to ensure they hoovered up all the big clubs that a cup format may filter out. Despite the huge cash incentives on offer (€6m for Barcelona and Real Madrid, and €3m for Atletico Madrid), the tournament only went ahead after the Saudis graciously allowed women to attend the games. Even their agreement to permit women feels medieval. Why should it be their choice to make? I watched the dramatic semi-final between Real Madrid and Barcelona with its five goals and 98-minute winner by Madrid's Federico Valverde and, although there were officially 35,000 fans there with 32,000 empty seats, the atmosphere was better in my front room as fans sat scrolling through their phones wondering why they had been told to come and watch this game that most of them had little interest in.

In glorious contrast was the same fixture based in the Nou Camp that saw tickets sold out in 72 hours to create a new record crowd for the women's game. The Champions League quarter-final between the teams that served up such drama to so many disinterested fans and empty seats now meant something more than a cash drop for Gerard Pique and his grubby associates. The women usually play at the club's training ground stadium that holds only 6,000 fans, so the change to a 90,000-capacity one speaks volumes for the integrity and huge momentum of the women's game. Their first Nou Camp game had been behind closed doors, in early 2021, so this felt like the real breakthrough. On 30 March 2022 the Nou Camp was packed when 91,533 fans (more than the men's Clasico and beating a 23-year-old record of 90,195 from the 1999 Women's World Cup in the United States) came to watch Barcelona Women beat Real Madrid Women 5-2 on the night and 8-3 overall in a pulsating, skill-packed Champions League quarter-final. Goosebumps came as standard when, rather than showing 'more than a club' in Spanish letters across the main stand, fans shared 'More Than Empowerment'. Although important to acknowledge the crowd of 110,000 for the women's World Cup Final in Mexico in 1971, this astonishing Catalan evening was the calling card for the push and pull factors at play. Writing for Football365. com on 4 May 2022, even my favourite curmudgeon John Nicholson couldn't help being swept away in the joy that this latest breach of the grass ceiling ushered in.

'That 91,000 at Barcelona didn't turn up to watch women's football per se, they turned up because it was Barcelona and Barcelona fans support Barcelona whoever they're playing. And that's as it should be.'

Closer to home, on 1 May 2022, Newcastle United Women played their first ever game at St James' Park and were rewarded not only by a 4-0 victory over Alnwick Town, but by an astonishing crowd of 22,134. If that wasn't mind-blowing enough, this was to watch a National League Division One North game which it blew away that season's highest attendance by almost 2,000 for the Women's Super League game between Manchester United and Everton. The start of the game even had to be delayed by 15 minutes to let all the fans in. 'Howay the lasses' indeed. This shows the magnetic pull of a rapidly developing, vibrant women's game and the push from an increasingly politicised world of men's football pursuing an American model of hermetically sealed franchise competition where success is open only to a privileged few.

***

The 2022 Women's Euros not only helped build profile and mark progress for the women's game but offered an ecosystem of opportunity. And what an ecosystem it was. On 11 May at the UEFA Congress, the head of women's football Nadine Kessler projected that the 2022 Euros would be broadcast to over 250 million people in 165 territories. A historic moment had finally arrived. As a tournament, its legacy will be driven by on-field success, but there is a much broader brief. The stars have finally aligned where increased profile, sponsorship, support and structure helps write women's football's next chapter and how the beautiful game can speak of wider societal issues that women have been short-changed on for centuries. If these women can excel in an environment of opportunity, then why can't every woman fighting an uphill battle just to be heard get the same chances?

Opportunity creates pathways that are established and open for other women to follow. The arch and 'half-decent football magazine' *When Saturday Comes* saw the opportunity to create new chances for women in late 2021 when it launched its mentoring scheme:

'Have you always wanted to write for *WSC*, or wondered what goes on behind closed doors at an independent football magazine? Do you want to learn new skills, make industry contacts and be paid to write an article that will be published in *WSC* magazine? We are excited to launch the first *WSC* mentoring and development scheme for aspiring and early-career female journalists, not currently in full-time education, with an interest in football/sports journalism. The scheme is free to take part in, and is open to ambitious writers, editors, sub-editors, podcasters and publishers, with a passion for football and something to say.'

Aiming to highlight and address the 'chronically under-represented' views of women, *WSC* offered a meaningful and structured process. The three-month course that started in early 2022 included a dozen hours of Zoom sessions, time with the key content producers, learning how to pitch content, sub-editing, podcasting and, finishing at the end of March 2022, production and business advice. After the course ended, the mentee was then invited back to help build a tailored career plan and have the chance to go through the whole creation, editing, pitching process to the journalists and finish with their own, paid article in the magazine with professional credits. These are the kind of initiatives that will create meaningful traction for lifelong opportunities.

For on-pitch and in-class opportunities, Barnsley's Women's Shadow Scholarship Open Training was a great example of small but meaningful steps to building profile and expanding opportunities. Not only can girls study on a Level 3 Sports Coaching or Level 3 Sports Science course, but they train three times a week, have access to technology to analyse their performance and they will continue to play for their regular weekend team to help spread the good practice they have learnt. The course was opened in February 2022 and the first cohort started later that year. Small, meaningful and measurable. These are small steps to mighty progress.

The Euros create a supermassive version of the *WSC* scheme if the opportunity is woven into the process of engaging, empowering, upskilling and mentoring women in the huge range of experiences the event offers. There are of course the high-profile roles like commentators, coaches and officials where progress to parity is being made. But a tournament ecosystem offers meaningful opportunities to make connections, develop those you already have and tempt back any who have decided not to renew agreements. The draw is a solid set-piece to bring together sponsors, ambassadors of the game and generate press coverage. Thankfully, the women's version went smoothly under the highly skilled stewardship of Gabby Logan and Alex Scott, unlike the men's Champions League draw in December 2021 that had to be sheepishly repeated. The draw sets the tone for a tournament and there was collegial confidence in their packed Mancunian venue. Getting the front-row support of men like David James, a man not known for his open-mindedness as a player but someone who has quietly transitioned to a mature and thoughtful supporter of the women's game, was also a big boost for the event. Inviting local team Formby Community FC was also a piece of productive PR that centred the focus on inclusivity. By the end of the 40-minute show, there was a feeling of real momentum as we came to the end of October 2021 and acres of clips and snippets to inspire girls and women to spread the word, take part and join their local club had been created.

Having highly successful and articulate ambassadors confidently on-message also helped to drive the narrative. Talking to UEFA, Denmark's double centurion of international caps, Katrine Pedersen, highlighted the progress in the game's skillsets. 'The game is constantly developing – it's getting quicker, the quality of the passing, the speed in both the actions and decision-making, tactically and the flexibility within the team, just as we see in men's football.'

For Sweden's Lotta Schelin, it was the choice of England and the passion we have for the game that were the tournament's unique selling points.

'Staging this tournament in England with huge stadiums like Wembley and Old Trafford is really, really important. We believe in what we can achieve in the women's game, and you can see that in England. At the Olympics in 2012, you saw the stadiums full, and it's kind of amazing to know that it's possible for these capacities to be filled up.'

What this tournament has seized that is often taken for granted by the men's versions is that the game is a showcase of personal qualities for successfully navigating our war-torn and contagious world. The Show Your Heart campaign was blended into the pre-tournament promotion and focussed on how the game's top players need 'grit, determination and heart' to keep moving forward. This is another trait that will chime with fans when Neymar Junior's private jets or Ronaldo's £370,000 watch create a Kardashian universe of ugly and pointless consumption. The organisers took these qualities on the road with the trophy to train their resources on each of the host cities, a smart move given their relatively limited range compared to the men's game. Like Her Game Too, they have identified education as a key tool to begin to change the current, often ugly narrative that this book's appendix shares in all its sordid detail. With a tight deadline of 2024 set by UEFA (are you watching Cop 26?) to show progress in participation, coaching and refereeing, benchmarks act as baselines for the present and ways to add value in the future. Each city is asked to take up the challenge of improving female opportunity under three key performance indicators. The decision to use equality, diversity, inclusivity helps the story of women to sit in the mature process that clubs around the country are already supporting, instead of trying to reinvent the wheel.

Mid-January 2022 saw the launch of the UEFA Women's EURO 2022 Schools Programme focussing on seven- to 14-year-old students in Key Stages 2 and 3. It made available a range of free resources grouped together into Challenge Packs containing two dozen short and high-impact activities in three key areas.

- Learn through cross-curricular activities about players and teams in the tournament and evaluating the media created before, around and after the tournament.
- Play to encourage activity, communication and a sense of fun, like choreographing a new goal celebration.
- Support by debates, research of a key theme in women's football and designing a new kit for their school team.

19.

A Woman's Place is in the Home Dressing Rooms

AS THE post-match interviews began to wind down after Leicester City's smash and grab victory over Liverpool on 28 December 2021, unprompted, Brendan Rodgers took the opportunity to praise another professional: 'I've obviously never met Emma [Hayes] before ... She's done an amazing job for women's football. All the things that you're doing are really helping women's football progress. As a fellow coach, watching from outside, you've done amazing.'

This is the type of broad-based reaction that not only highlights a stellar career for Hayes, but models the type of behaviour Rogers expects from Foxes fans. It may have come across as low-key, but it hit all the right notes.

But Rogers remains something of an outlier. Women's football has often faced apathy, ridicule and aggression during the last century and a half. Former Aston Villa chairman Doug Ellis once odiously shared why he paid himself a handsome wage from the Villa Park kitty:

'Only women and horses work for nothing.'

Even now, with their game enjoying exponential growth turbocharged by this summer's Euros in England, a depressingly old-fashioned attitude to their participation in the beautiful game lingers from some of its male, pale and stale custodians. But, increasingly, beacons of hope are being built. Founded on a 'one club' policy, Chelsea has shown how supporting the women's game brings benefits for everyone. Talking to *The Guardian*'s Louise Taylor in May 2021, the Blues' manager Hayes (a woman who blew away many of her fellow male commentators during the 2020 Euros with her insight and tactical awareness) highlighted the enlightened philosophy that helped both club teams reach their respective Champions League finals:

'This is the most special club in the world because of both its diversity and its togetherness as a whole.'

Hayes was awarded an MBE in the 2016 Honours List, and her incredible intelligence and universal respect was rewarded in the 2022 list with an OBE. Her tweet in response showed all the class and gravitas of a beacon of good practice to drive the women's game forward:

'All I can say is thank you. To the whole women's football community, we are getting there. Keep pushing and girls and women across the country will keep getting recognised for our love for the beautiful game. To @ChelseaFCW you are my family. I love you all.'

Of course, Hayes has an incredibly high profile in the game and on our screens, but it was also heartening that England's first female captain received an MBE this year. Sheila Parker was, like Lily Parr, a player for Dick, Kerr Ladies. Gail Newsham, who gave me invaluable insight for the chapter on Lily, described the honour as 'richly deserved'.

Another hopeful development for 2021 came at AC Milan where, for the first time in Serie A history, a women's team debuted a club's home kit, when AC Milan's Women's team played Sassuolo on 25 May. Not only did they get to unveil the kit but they have their own shirt sponsor to promote their team as a member of the Milan family rather than a cast-off of the men's team.

There was also a nice touch to remind us of how far the women's game has come despite the restrictions placed on it by men. The FA confirmed that the 51st Women's FA Cup Final would be played at Wembley on Sunday, 5 December 2021, marking the 100th anniversary of its ban on women's football on the same day in 1921.

But the wider game still has so much to learn. Writing in May 2021 for *The Guardian*, Lousie Taylor perceptively wrote:

'Some WSL teams are still treated as second-, or even third-class citizens in comparison to their sibling men's sides but Roman Abramovich, Chelsea's [former] owner, has always had time for Hayes, and her squad's achievements represent much more than a footnote in Stamford Bridge history.'

In Michael Calvin's *State of Play*, Hayes described the different culture in the women's game:

'Culturally, women's football has an endearing innocence. There's less cynicism,' Hayes confirms with a chuckle. 'Do you think I can get my goalkeeper to fucking fall over and get the physio on the pitch so that I can get some information out there? She can't do it. She's too honest.'[15]

***

There now appears an unstoppable momentum towards male and female parity. In May 2021 the English FA made a timely and elegant tweak to its national team crest: replacing the three male lions with a lion, lioness and cub aims to reflect what its press release described as, 'progression, greater inclusivity and accessibility in all levels of the beautiful game; from grassroots to elite'. It was a classy move by an organisation not previously renowned for its innovation or modern outlook.

---

15 Calvin, M. *State of Play* pp. 132-133, (Random House. Kindle Edition).

The rising momentum around the women's game was finally acknowledged by Nike prior to the 2019 Women's World Cup. For the first time the company designed shirts specifically for women rather than tossing across the men's cast-offs. 'We believe this summer can be another turning point for the growth of women's football,' said Nike president and CEO Mark Parker.

'Our bigger ambition is for that energy and participation to extend into all sports. Nike's commitment is to continue our leading support of competitive athletes, invest in the next generation at the grassroots level and deliver more innovative and compelling product design for women,' he explained.

Nike started with the previous all-white England kit and added some stylish touches, like red cuffs. 'The flood-white look gives an aura of strength and purity. This minimalism translates as sophistication and confidence – perfect for this team,' according to Cassie Looker, Nike women's football apparel lead. Rather than be picked up off the men's production line, this kit was designed after 4D scanning of the players at the Nike Sports Research Lab and each kit was made using more than a dozen recycled plastic bottles to tie in with Nike's sustainability drive that has used over six million plastic bottles in its products since 2010.

***

But, depressingly, misogynistic dinosaurs still roam the earth. In 2004 Sepp Blatter showed his true Neanderthal colours when announcing that women should 'wear tighter shorts and low-cut shirts to create a more female aesthetic'. This from a man with a daughter. Appalling.

Reporting for *The Guardian* in October 2020, journalist Suzanne Wrack also analysed some depressing conclusions. Two-thirds of women working in football have experienced gender discrimination in the workplace, according to Women in Football's biggest survey. Talking to 4,200 women in the organisation, the WiF chair, Ebru Köksal, described the results as 'heartbreaking and devastating'. Former referee Janie Frampton illustrated the depressing situation too often faced by female players and officials:

'Myself and Wendy Toms were the first two women [referees] that came through the men's professional game in the 90s. Both of us have said so many times since that we probably had too high a tolerance level at the time because we just wanted to fit in. Now, we've come on 30 years and we are still experiencing the same issues ... Wendy and I were treated as a circus – I don't want that to still be the case now.'

As you might have noticed, I'm a big fan of how Hamburg's St Pauli do things, and this continues with their attitude to women. They are the European club with the biggest proportion of female fans in the stadium for match days, with 30 per cent joining in the 'Millerntor Roar'. Of course, Germany is seen as an enlightened political and social country, but let's not forget that until 30 October 1970, the German Football Association prohibited women from playing. Astonishing. I suppose when your language describes male and female teams as mannschaft, which comes from the German word for man (mann) we shouldn't be so surprised. But, as Michael Calvin explains, it was just as depressingly regressive in England:

'Women's football has survived scarcely credible ignorance; it was banned by the FA for 50 years, until 1971. FIFA's veneer of inclusivity was exposed by President Gianni Infantino, who welcomed delegates to a conference in Zurich in March 2018 on the theme of "Making Equality a Reality" less than 24 hours after attending the Tehran derby, from which female spectators were banned.'[16]

---

16   Calvin, M. *State of Play* p. 129, (Random House. Kindle Edition).

Scaling the paywall

The profile of the women's game and a showcase for the players and their kits recently received a much-deserved turbo boost. In March 2021, an agreement was signed between the FA, Sky and the BBC to co-ordinate coverage of the WSL. Sky's paywall is problematic for viewing figures, but they have the funds women's football needs. However, the profile which the BBC brings with it, over and above the peppering of highlights and occasional cup matches for the men's game, is a big leap forward. John Nicholson sees the huge platform and viewing figures generated by the last Women's World Cup as compelling evidence to scale the paywall alienating the men's game from the majority of fans:

'Right now, there is a palpable shift of mood against sports being available only behind paywalls. The Women's World Cup has been a huge TV success this summer, pulling 11.7 million people in to watch England's semi-final on the BBC. With talk turning to how the women's game is going to develop in the future, many have expressed fear that it will be bought by Sky.'[17]

Shown on terrestrial TV, the tournament pulled in numbers that Sky could never reach for England games. The quarter-final against Norway attracted 6.1 million to 7.4 million viewers and there were 11.7 million for the semi-final against the USA. This has proved to be the engine driving the new TV deal. It's a three-year agreement that pulls in around £8m annually starting in the 2021-22 season, making it the world's biggest female sports broadcast deal. Of course, that represents less than Sky pays for broadcasting a single Premier League game, but this deal is structured so much more sustainably than the madness of needing to generate £9.3m to break even for a Fulham against Brighton snorefest.

---

17 Nicholson, J. *Can We Have Our Football Back?: How the Premier League is ruining football and what we can do about it* p. 10, (Head Publishing. Kindle Edition).

Shown across the three platforms of Sky, BBC and the FA Player, fans get weekly access to matches to help build the brand. Two weekly fixtures will be on Sky, one on the BBC and a total of 75 games shown on the FA Player through the season. The shop window is now fully visible for fans to start perusing what is inside.

20.

The Future's So Bright
We Gotta Wear Shades

'Things are going great, and they're
only getting better
I'm doing all right, getting good grades
The future's so bright I gotta wear shades.'

Timbuk-3

LAUNCHED AT the start of the 2021/22 season, Women of Watford remains the Premier League's only female supporters' group. It was formed by Kate Lewers who, on 22 January 2022 on the BBC's *Football Focus* passionately and intelligently explain why her group was needed, WOW reflects Kate's own frustrations and the challenges of trying to support the club she loves.

Like Her Game Too, the group aims to give women a louder voice in the club, encourage and celebrate a more diverse fan base and inspire future generations of women to play, watch and work in football. It also provides a sense of community and security for women watching Watford where they can enjoy matches together and serve as role models for young girls at the match to show that women matter. Kate told Watford's social media team:

'In March I appeared on *Hive Live* to celebrate International Women's Day and discuss being a female fan. One question I was asked really made me think: how do I feel as a woman attending away games? I suddenly realised I had never, and most likely never would, go to an away game by myself.

'That same week saw the death of Sarah Everard at the hands of a stranger as she was walking home in the dark, prompting many women to share their own stories of being followed or simply not doing something they would like out of fear for their own safety.

'We welcome all who agree with our aims, regardless of gender identity. We stand for community, allyship and diversity amongst plenty of other things and, if you relate to that and want to ensure Watford FC is a positive experience for all, we'd love to have you with us.'

The word 'allyship' is key. It is not enough to give women a sense of security through a female-formed community. The men behaving appallingly need to confront and question their own behaviour, self-police and empathise with their own fans who are being intimidated, isolated and driven out of the game. Every step WOW makes and every moment a man reflects on his words and actions that could demean and depress another fan, the closer we will be to concentrating on the big issues together as a unified fanbase, such as why the linesman should have gone to Specsavers or how the referee always gives soft free kicks against us.

While there remain huge areas of concern for groups like Her Game Too to address in the game (many of which are heartbreakingly highlighted in the appendix), it's really important to finish this chapter of the women's game with some of the extremely positive steps being taken.

On 15 December 2021 the FA agreed to a £30m deal for women's football that will run until 2025. The deal also coupled with the strong High Street-brand power of Barclays.

Two years previously they had created Barclays Girls' Football School Partnerships, which aimed to give girls in English schools equal access to football by 2024. This was supported by Barclays Game On, a scheme to use football as a way to teach life skills to girls in school. This is a strategy echoed by Her Game Too, where Caz, Lucy and the team engage with girls at school using links created through club trusts.

So, the new commitment Barclays made in 2021 was part of a strategy rather than a short-term tactic. The agreement also saw a community fund being launched for the girls' and women's grassroots game. This is something that I, a sponsor of Exeter City Women's Zoe Watkins, have found most striking. The sheer volume of goodwill, collegiality and excitement in women's football is contagious and not something I see every week in my local men's teams. There's a spirit of the pioneer within evolving football and this is clearly something Barclays has noticed and, like any good business, it has seen a business opportunity to address. When 50 per cent of any population is poorly served, it is not only a weakness but also an opportunity.

Writing in *The Guardian*, Suzanne Wrack highlighted how this is not a new initiative, but a doubling of Barclays' previous commitment to the game. Two years earlier Barclays became the WSL's first title sponsor, and now its profile is evolving in a more meaningful way than simply looking to add funds to the already well-resourced top-tier teams. Looking back on the explosion of women's football since 2019, Barclays clearly hit an investment sweet spot of the big bang moment for the women's game and in hindsight will see the return on its investment as handsome. As Wrack illustrates:

'Since Barclays became title sponsor of the WSL and backed the FA Girls' Football School Partnership, which aims to give girls equal access to football in schools, 9,700 schools have joined the scheme taking the total to over 12,000 and the ambition is to reach girls at 90 per cent of primary and secondary schools in the UK.'

What also gives this partnership profile and heft is that it runs parallel to Barclays' ongoing commitment to the men's game, even if the figures are very different. The 2021 deal was thought to double the previous £6m agreement, which didn't include marketing or prize money. Their total investment with the FA is £30m.

Late 2021 also saw the FA reveal its latest three-year strategy for growing the women's professional game in England. The 32-page report has a bold aim, especially when you look at the ambitious aims in the American women's game of developing 'the best women's leagues in the world'. The three key drivers in the report are: to create, attract and secure the world's best players; to capture, engage and monetise fans; and to put in place a lucrative but sustainable strategy for growing commercial revenue.

There are a series of helpful milestones baked into the plan that will test and evaluate progress to avoid some of the mistakes being made in the men's games. A talent pipeline needs to be productive but must also be made up of a sustainable blend of homegrown and imported talent. Targeting a minimum of 50 per cent of head coaches across the top divisions being female seems to me like a halfway house decision. When top female coaches are given opportunities in the senior men's game, then it would be good to see this aim slide and coaches simply being qualified based on their skills rather than their gender. But, for now, this is a necessary protection for the female coaches like Helen Nkwocha, studying hard for their qualifications and sacrificing time and finances in the hope of being given future opportunities.

The attendance targets are a motivating stretch and have an aim to average 6,000 fans in the WSL by 2024. Considering the average for the 2021/22 season was 2,282 and that this represented a downward trend (of course, Covid always has to be considered here), for most clubs to be selling out their current stadiums in three years is a mighty ask. Luckily, the 2022 Euros are likely to give figures a big boost, particularly if the home nations advance to the latter stages or win the competition outright.

What is highly attractive about this strategy is how this on-field and in-stadium growth is seen as the platform to help girls and women grow careers within and around the game. Making the women's game a platform for female role models, encouraging more active lifestyles and all the mental health benefits of being part of a thriving women's game is key. This was supported by partnerships with organisations like United Minds FC, the club based in Sunderland who use their games as ways to help promote better mental wellbeing. The game can share a voice in driving more social equality, that seems to have been beaten out of the top levels of the men's game by vampiric agents, obscene wages and (notable exceptions like Marcus Rashford aside) lifestyles lived for Instagram, not to help make a more equitable society.

Acknowledgements

THE INSPIRATION for writing this book came from the indefatigable founders of Her Game Too. Caz and Lucy have shown limitless grace under pressure and, when needed, sheer bloody-mindedness that has blown me away. But the biggest inspiration for writing, or indeed getting out of bed in the morning, comes from my long-suffering wife Karen.

Anyone who has tried to navigate getting a book to market knows that writing it is often the easy part. With other projects, I have been kept waiting for months on end for even the shortest of replies and strung along with glowing terms that have slowly turned to ashes. Jane Camillin at Pitch Publishing has been helpful, honest and disarmingly frank. I can't thank or recommend Pitch enough. Laura Wolfe's passionate championing of the women's game was yet another Pitch-fuelled inspiration. There was a great deal of interest in this book from agents and other publishers after the fact, but Pitch Publishing is the place for me and I hope to repay company with strong book sales and not too many spelling mistakes!

Huge thanks to my editor Katie Field whose thoughtful and forensic suggestions have hopefully turned my mediocre prose into something you enjoyed.

A big thanks to the Exeter City media crew of Craig, Scott and Jed for all their help and advice. They do an immense job of promoting the club as one – male and female – and were at the vanguard of partnering with Her Game Too. Thanks also to Chad Gribble at Exeter City Women FC and especially to their official photographer Neil Richardson for taking the fantastic photos you see. Exeter City really are a special club and I'm honoured to be a season ticket holder and Trust member. Grateful thanks to Roberto Petrucco for allowing me to share his interview with Lucy.

Gail Newsham was a real help getting insight into the true story of Lily Parr (something that many other authors have failed to discover).

Thanks also go to Nial Couper at Fair Game UK for his relentless drive to infuse football with sustainability, integrity and community. I also really appreciate the support of two of the Fair Game UK directors, Christina Philippou and Natalie Atkinson; with their passionate and imaginative ideas for bringing parity to football for all, they have given me extra motivation when the writing deadlines have had me flagging. Thanks so much too for Helen Nkwocha's time and the passionate story she shared.

Ric from Hope and Glory Merchandise and Scott from NI Mug Co were kind enough to keep me up to speed with developments and provide some impressive images for their great range of goods to help spread awareness of Her Game Too. Thanks also go to the United Mates Football Podcasts, Craig Beazley from the AFC Bournemouth Fans Channel and Vital Walsall for sharing their interviews with Caz and Lucy, to James at Bristol Rovers for his help and access to some top Rovers-related images andto Chris Hull, the Nationwide Respect ambassador who also works for Sky Sports. Cameron Cairns is owed a thank you for sharing his interview with HGT co-founder Amy Clement, as is Jo Kinney from Ignite Soccer Agency for her time and insight.

The Her Game Too Survey

#HERGAMETOO
Sexist Abuse in Football Survey
June 2021

371 responses from women in the UK

We then asked, 'if you have answered yes to any of the above, and you feel comfortable doing so, please share your experiences with us'. Below are the results. We wanted to select a few to share but we think the sheer volume really says something and confirms why #HerGameToo is necessary. It is quite overwhelming to read. WARNING: bad language.

'I mainly find it occurs in pubs when watching football. My opinions aren't validated because I'm female. I've had to leave pubs because of arguments etc that have occurred. Quite often it's the same insult "what do you know, you're a girl?", "go cook something", "isn't there some cleaning to do somewhere?"'

'Most abuse is online and follows the general "who let you out of the kitchen?" type comments when I've disagreed with a man about something football related. I've also had someone ask me if I'm on my period because I didn't share their views and got upset with their sexist comments.'

'Remarks such as "you're a woman, what do you know?" or "oh you like football, tell me the offside rule."'

'Regularly told to "go back to the kitchen" etc on football Twitter for having an opinion. Or called names like "slag" or "whore" or "dumb bitch". Also received unsolicited pictures or unwanted advances in DMs.'

'Just comments such as "oh you know a lot about football for a girl" or "how come you like football?"'

'My experience of a football fan of Peterborough United has been amazing! We have a lot of female fans and I hope that I'm not in the minority when I say that there is very little discrimination. I do think the football landscape has changed a lot over the years (I've been going 25 years) and there have been very few incidents where I felt uncomfortable – I'd say these are mostly from opposing fans and from a long time ago.'

'I go with my male partner and his comments and views are acknowledged but I'm generally ignored so I usually just keep quiet. We're seated with other season ticket holders so see the same people every match. It's not overt but it is demeaning. Of the two of us I'm definitely more knowledgeable than my spouse!'

'A lot of dismissive attitudes – it's like your opinion isn't valued just because you're a woman. Or, if you express you know anything, men often act with surprise and it's really condescending. There's also seeing other women online get abuse ("get back in the kitchen") or just general creepy behaviour from male fans. Finally, people expressing that you're only into football to impress men and because you fancy the players! Everything is just so frustrating.'

'I've been told to go shopping a number of times whilst watching non-league football, by a club manager and a fellow spectator.'

'It all started at school about three years ago when some of the boys found out that I liked watching football and the team I supported. When I tried to get involved in conversations about football, they would constantly ask me questions such as "do you even know the offside rule?" and say things such as "you only like football to try and get men's attention". Following that I kept my opinions on football quiet for a little while.

'When I joined Twitter, I received the same sort of comments just for simply tweeting my opinions on a Manchester United game. I've been told a number of times that I can't support Manchester United just because I'm a woman and "I know nothing about the game and should just get back in the kitchen".'

'Just general comments that we don't understand the rules and that I only like football because how attractive the players are.'

'Abuse about not knowing the rules, wolf whistled at whilst walking to games, jeered by competitor fans at away matches, seen online abuse and opinions argued with for no reason except women don't know the answers.'

'At a children's football match, I was told by an opposition parent to, "get off to the shopping centre" as I don't belong at a football match.'

'Just on social media people making comments about girls "pretending" to watch football and just pretending to like it to get a guy's attention.'

'Whilst leaving an away game at Spurs, wearing my Norwich scarf, I was told to "watch it, you slag" by a Spurs fan. I was on my own. I became incredibly anxious, keeping my head down and walking as fast as I could through heaving crowds of Spurs fans. I took off my scarf so as not to attract attention to myself.'

'There have always been grey areas of men online being patronising about my football opinions. I remember the Karen Carney incident at Christmas when there was a load of abuse sent to her and she left Twitter because of it.'

'Sexist comments. I take my children (seven-year-olds) to games and when explaining things, I have been interrupted by people we don't know because they think they know better. It scares my children, so we stopped going to 'big' grounds and stick to grassroots games.'

'I've been told that we aren't worthy of an opinion as it's a man's game.'

'I believe the mindset was set in schools, as at my school I was told by teachers that football was a boys' game and I'd much prefer to dance.'

'Honestly, I feel like I have had very few experiences directly aimed at me, but that I witness microaggressions at almost every game: if there's a female official, when there's a female pundit on Sky, etc.'

'Told to get out of football, I don't belong at a game.'

'Got shouted at by Chelsea fans to get my boobs out and when I said no and walked off, they shouted "get back to the kitchen then".'

'Watching the Arsenal v Liverpool FA Cup Final match in 2001 in a pub on my own because I was away for the weekend and none of my pals I was with were interested in it. Plenty of smutty comments, too many to list especially when Arsenal went ahead. Met a nice gang of lads who knew I was only trying to enjoy the footie and looked after me from the mob.'

'During my A-Levels I told my guidance councillor that I was going to Uni to study sports journalism and I was told that I should change my degree because that's too hard for girls to get into and it isn't "what they do". I graduated with a first, currently doing my masters in it and working for two radio stations.'

'I went to collect my match accreditation at the media stand and me and a man turned up at the same time, they asked him all the usual questions, I got asked twice if I was the cleaner. After arriving upstairs to be shown to the press area I was asked if I was sure I was meant to be there when none of my male colleagues were asked the same.'

'Regularly asked if I actually know anything about football, am I just here because I fancy the players.'

'I politely called out a football fan of an opposition team for using the term "gay" in a pejorative manner and he responded by criticising my appearance.'

'I am very careful about what I tweet about football as I have seen the abuse other women can receive when they do so. I do try to show support to those who have been abused.'

'I have been called a "dyke" by opposition male fans for attending football matches, on more than one occasion. I find it offensive that men use the word as a term of abuse.'

'I used to run the line for my son's football team (usually because none of the fathers would do it). This happened in a cup final and pre-match, the ref asked me if I knew the offside rule. He did not ask the father from the opposition the same question. I was so taken aback I just meekly replied "yes". I so regret not retorting "of course, do you need me to explain it to you?" or at least asking him to ask the dad the same thing.'

'I was told to go back to the kitchen because women "don't know anything about football".'

'Basic sexist messages about not knowing anything about football, my opinion being irrelevant. That I must be a lesbian. Telling me to just shut up.'

'Not really at the pub or a game as the fans I sit with are all welcoming and don't care about gender as long as you're wearing blue and white stripes. At school and collage definitely experienced it especially when I was knowledgeable about which players were in form etc. Lads always acted surprised I knew as much if not more than them, which makes me feel like I have to go above and beyond in order to prove I'm a "real" football fan.'

'When I've shared an opinion on football, if there's any negative responses, 95 per cent of them are to do with my gender/looks. "Ugly c*nt so she has to pretend to like football to attract a man…" '

'At games, in person, told to pop behind the bar at half time to do something useful, like get in a kitchen to sort out food and drinks for the "proper fans" (men).'

'In the pub I have had men tell me to shut up when I've expressed an opinion.'

'At the match I've heard other supporters abusing a female lines-person.'

'I get patronised on social media occasionally, as though my opinions don't matter because I'm a woman. It's usually older men who do it with the odd "maybe you should stick to (enter stereotypical pastimes here)" or "explain to me how you came to that conclusion darling/love/sweetheart" but most of the time it's respectful interaction.'

'People questioning my interest for football. Saying I am only doing it for attention. Asking if I know certain players or rules. The list goes on and on.'

'General comments like "why are you here you're a girl, get back in the kitchen, why do you play football it's a boys' sport, do you even know the rules? Why do you play football, surely you can't be very good?"'

'I follow my local club as well as a premier league side. At non-league games I have suffered. Been told to shut up. Go home. Don't know what you're talking about.'

'I get told that my opinion is not valid. I am seen as a lower "class" in the football fan system. I'm told to "get back to the kitchen" or "I don't belong in this game" or I am asked to prove myself to other male fans.

'I've been told to stick to making sandwiches and googling the attractive players names, I have also been told that I'm too young to understand football especially considering I'm a woman. I wrote some positive feedback about a player's performance and was told I was just a fan girl. My club won a match before and some of the fanbase told me I was too positive about it so I clearly don't know football.'

'I've seen Karen Carney and Alex Scott get abuse over social media countless times. I get abuse usually in Twitter DMs and it's people telling me I know nothing, to get back in the kitchen and my opinion is shite. When I'm refereeing, I feel like I get more targeted abuse towards my gender then my male counterparts do.'

'Football's a men's topic, you get back to your make-up stuff.'

'I'm sure you watch it for hot footballers.'

'Especially early on when I was going to games and interacting with others, people would ignore me and whatever I had to say and just talk to my brother and dad. On social media it is usually that I don't "understand" the game in the way the men do.'

'I have seen a lot more sexism online than in person. Thankfully where I sit and watch football I know the people who sit around me and I have never heard any sexist abuse from them. I have heard it once or twice towards a female official though.'

'I've seen regular abuse aimed at female commentators/ pundits online.'

'Twitter can be an interesting place sometimes, I regularly see negative comments sent to women who work in football, comment on football. Largely by the male population. Times need to change.'

'I have witnessed female friends receiving abuse before matches.'

'At the stadium I am surrounded by men, and especially when Sian Massey has been on the line for us there is cat calling and any time she gets a decision "wrong" it's because she's a woman.'

'Wow, where do I start!!'

'There were several remarks made to me during matches when I was around 10, but I thought this was just normal. Just little remarks here and there.'

'It was only when I began working in the football industry as media that the bad abuse came. My first experience was with a man a few years older than me (I was 16 at the time) who began speaking to me at the game while we were both photographing the game – which quickly progressed to remarks about my body, and what he "would like to do with me" – obviously chat which isn't pleasant when trying to work!

'Worse than that, it was someone I trusted next. Like really trusted. My boss at the club who was in charge of media would regularly text me to ask me how I was and how my day was going (there was a 20-year age gap, but he gained my trust quickly). This really quickly escalated into grooming behaviour, trying to isolate me from my family, and would frequently gather info about me. When he became sexual, and would send me inappropriate images, I began to think this was wrong and threatened to tell people. What was even more disconcerting is that for the next football match (this was during lockdown) he had a graphic and well-prepared plan for how he would have sex with me in the grounds during the game. It was absolutely awful. I began to tell people, and he found out, and began telling what I was allowed to say, and what not to say about him. It is sorted now, but in the end, I have been kicked out of the club I supported for my life when he is able to keep working there.

'I still feel scared and embarrassed around men, so much so I have developed a tremor and feel unable to return to any football matches in future. I'm also scared to be alone in the city where my boss may be able to find me, and even now I am scared to tell my story in case he finds it!'

'I've been asked to move tables so "real" (in their eyes male) fans can watch games, asked if I know about football to make my boyfriend happy and have a ridiculous number of men over the years demand that I explain the offside rule as if to prove I'm not lying when I say that I know and love football.'

'Sexist comments are regularly made about female physios on the pitch.'

'My own personal social media isn't too bad … but in 2020 I was regularly appearing on various YouTube football streams where the live chat comments would sometimes be derogatory towards me as a woman. Suggesting I didn't have a right to be a fan or even work in sport because I'm a woman.'

'My grassroots team was the first ever female fan team to go on *SoccerAM* and the comments were horrendous and sexist.'

'I've received messages on Twitter from a troll saying I give female football fans a bad name and that I'm obsessed with certain players and only copy other people's views.'

'I've been called a bitch by an away fan when leaving Roots Hall, and after a Southend away game I have also been called a slag; both of these happened when I was about 15/16 years old.'

'When watching a football match on a TV before, someone commented that they didn't know why I was watching it and that my opinion didn't matter and that I wasn't really interested in football, but they soon stopped when I said I had a season ticket at Southend.'

'Asked whether I was taken to matches by a boyfriend. And do I like football because I fancy the players?'

'Just conversations with male counterparts really laughing at the fact I play football as a female. Being told I have a better place in the kitchen.'

'More so from telling people that I play – most people love the fact that women play football, but I've had the occasional comments that it is a "men's" sport and that women shouldn't play. It's the shock on some people's faces too when I actually know what I'm talking about when discussing football! 90 per cent of the time though, I do have a positive experience.'

'I am a budding football photographer and have been subject to sexist abuse on occasions.'

'I had a journalist at a paper tell me that I wouldn't get anywhere in football as I am a woman.'

'I work for a men's non-league football club, Hednesford Town FC. You become very accustomed to the wolf whistles, and I just take that in my stride. But one away game a group of home fans stood behind the dugout and for the entire game shouted sexual abuse at me, asking me to get my tits out, told me I belonged in the kitchen, shouted at me to jump up and down.'

'I would say mainly trolls on YouTube (I'm lucky, not too many to be honest). The usual nonsense comments. "Get back to the kitchen". "Why is a woman talking about football?" I usually just ignore, mute/block and move on.'

'Lame comments on Twitter about getting back to the kitchen and not having a clue about football.'

'Only ever received it at a pub!'

'Men making comments, "what would you know about football, you're only a girl!"'

'Don't talk about something you don't know anything about.'

'I went to my local to watch our first game in the Premier League (vs Liverpool) and I got so excited (and had also chugged two pints on an empty stomach) that I cried a bit when Jack Harrison scored the opener. There was a lad behind me who was also a Leeds fan and he got very excited too. An older bloke sat opposite me, who I later found out was a Newcastle fan, loudly told the pub that me crying was "exactly why women shouldn't watch football. Go watch it in the kitchen love." I was outraged and my (now ex) partner told me to shut up rather than loudly respond as I wanted to. He also always hated it when I got excited about football, often telling me to shut up if I cheered when we scored, despite him being a very loud Spurs fan.'

'Have been asked on multiple occasions if I actually "know the rules" despite being qualified as a ref. Have been laughed at for being at the game, asked to perform sexual acts on men in the toilets at half time.'

'While watching football and commenting on it (making suggestions on possible changes) I've had someone say "what do you know about football you're a girl?"'

'I have been verbally abused online and told that I don't know what I'm talking about because I'm a woman and in the local pub.'

'The typical "you're a woman what do you know? Shouldn't you be at home in the kitchen? Bet you only watch to look at the legs. How can you know anything you never played the game?"'

'Throughout my whole life. I once got called a "blonde bimbo" for expressing a football opinion on Twitter. Even if it's not expressly said – the condescension and "no one cares" attitude when it comes to women's football and not being taken seriously with my thoughts and wanting to play when I was younger.'

'My favourite is one that isn't abuse, just an unhelpful assumption. I met my boyfriend watching Rotherham and I've had people comment that it's nice he's got me to come along with him … he points out I've been going longer than him. My opinions on football generally are often dismissed by men, in which case I get quite competitive and like to show them that I see more live games than them (usually true, out of the context of football matches) or at least as many, and that I know what I'm talking about.'

'On the Everton Toffees fan club Twitter page, I ended up having to unfollow due to the terrible abuse and attacks I was getting every time I posted my thoughts or my opinion on the game which they didn't like … swore at me, called me names, so derogatory that I was in tears and my daughter posted a reply to them telling them to back off and that there was no need for their abuse and criticism … my 26-year-old daughter

... terrible. So that silenced me and excluded me. Who gives them the right to make degrading comments about me and basically word rape on a bloody football forum? I've been a fan all my life!! They just couldn't and can't take a pretty, strong woman having an opinion. Simple. It was always the same when I went the match to Goodison on my own ... I ended up stopping going it hurt me so much. Hanging up on me, making lewd remarks, telling me to shut the f up that I'm not qualified to pass comment ... me, a business director who has set up more than seven Everton supporters clubs across the world including Russia on my travels with work. I come back to this country to chauvinism, verbal and physical abuse, misogyny ... I ended up never going to the pub, never going to the game and not wearing my shirt or scarf out to not attract attention. Horrific.'

'Most of the abuse I have received has been what those giving it would consider "banter" – for example, "get back in the kitchen". But I've been made to feel like my opinion means less as a female.'

'One comment that stands out was made by another female actually, who said I pretended to like football to get boys' attention.'

'In our FPL Community on Twitter, I have seen women relentlessly mocked for an unpopular opinion or perceived "dumb" decision. Instead of letting each do their own, a guy once felt the need to post a very large unflattering image of the woman who stated the unpopular opinion with derogatory comments underneath. It was uncalled for, overly harsh, just a brutal thing to do. Her looks have nothing to do with her opinion, it was demeaning to post the unflattering photo with the caption underneath, reducing her to an object to be laughed at and publicly derided.'

'Have seen many nasty and rude comments especially on Twitter towards comments made about football from women. Unfortunately too many to put.'

'There are countless times I've been called a slag/bitch for saying something a man doesn't agree with. Also get back in the kitchen/make a sandwich etc. At an FA Cup game once, a man was making sexist comments when a player went down injured. When I confronted him about it, he was yelling in my face saying I was a silly little girl and what did I know?'

'I have received inappropriate sexual comments and also had my opinions mocked because I'm female.'

'I have been told I don't have a clue what's going on, I have been told that as long as I only watch and have an opinion on women's football then it's fine and I've been told to go back and do what women do best.'

'Violent sexual language directed towards me when I've had a difference of opinion eg "you fucking stupid slag".'

'Generic comments online about "women not knowing enough about football".'

'Some very dated remarks like "get back to the kitchen"', "leave it to the guys you don't know" – belittled for having an opinion. Regular ignorant comments mainly from my experience.'

'There are so many! I can't count the number of times I've got chatting to a guy in the pub and told them I'm a Spurs fan, and they say something like, "really, name three players then". A West Ham fan on Twitter called me a "clapped wh*re" because I posted a pic of the view from my seat and made a joke. I've had some sexual and disturbing comments made on YouTube livestreams about me when I've appeared on them. I could go on! I've been following Mel Seballos for a while and the abuse she got towards her, and her daughter were the worst I've seen. But women are always being harassed online – every female football fan on Twitter I've seen get DMs and comments from young guys, old guys, it doesn't matter, on their looks, their bodies etc and we just want to share our love for the game!'

'From general comments about women in the game to stating my view on the potential of players and being laughed at (then that player actually becomes excellent as I predicted with the right tactics). People not listening to my comments at the match then repeating it louder and men around agreeing. From being challenged about the offside rule. Sexual comments and focus on which player I fancy the most (to which I always asked that back).'

'I received lots of sensitive abuse when I played football, I also have witnessed people in pubs and on social media.'

'Watching football in person I have heard remarks such as "Women don't understand football".'

'I'm from the US but I've had so many instances throughout my life! By far the most toxic (and unoriginal) are on social media. You get the classic "stay in the kitchen. You only like it to attract guys, etc." or just plain disgusting stuff. The ones in person (bars/pubs/dates) are the more subtle, "oh you know a lot about sports for a girl" and other classic misogynistic things where they ask you some ridiculous sporting detail to "prove" you know sports.'

'Been told to go back to the kitchen. I shouldn't be at the game because I'm a girl. I can't play football because I'm a girl. I "know a lot about football" for a girl. Been called a lesbian because I play football. The list is endless.'

'I'm a coach for a local kids' session and I was kicking a ball to a dad back and forth a few times. He said "You've got good touch, for a woman" … Made me a little bit mad, cos I've been playing footy for five years (I would have given it up if I wasn't any good!)'.

'Suffered sexual assault at a football match.'

'Had chants to get my tits out "for the lads" from when I was as young as 14.'

'My opinions didn't matter because I was a girl, what did I know about football – turned out more than some of them arrogant male fans.'

'I'm a match-day volunteer and I've had sexist verbal abuse when walking through the away end

Being told I should be quiet and focus on "raising the lads' spirits" (cue winks/nudges/smirks) instead of talking about something I don't understand.'

'I've been called/referred to as: a daft bint; a dumb blonde; a silly young girl; tits with a gob; sweetheart/darling/love-in patronising tones.

'Fans at football grounds I find very welcoming from all genders however at pubs probably experience more sexist behaviour. I've been told I "just don't understand or get it" if my opinion is different and had to, on numerous occasions, justify why I support certain teams and getting questioned on how many times I go to games and when I state I'm a season ticket holder I then get questioned on how many away games I go to (bear in mind always in pubs or interacting online never at the game with other fans – which is why I chose not to state my opinion online as much).'

'Been sworn at on the terrace at home and away games for being a "f***ing woman". Also got asked if I was lost once.'

'Regularly asked if it's my first game. Do I even know the offside rule? OMG you're a woman who likes football, can

I marry you? Your husband is a lucky guy (because I like football).'

'When I was pregnant with my little boy (we didn't know what we were having) people kept saying to me – I bet you want it to be a boy so you can take it to football with you. I would then respond with "but I'm female and I go football?!?!"'

'Repeatedly been told I only watch football because I fancy the men. Asked if I was forced to go by my dad. Totally ignored if I made a point during a game, got my husband to make same point and he was told it was a great point.'

'Constantly being told that my opinion doesn't matter as I'm both young and a girl and also whilst playing I have had far too many people tell me I can't as I'm a girl and to go and make them a sandwich instead …

'Comments on Twitter about "'getting back to the kitchen" and it being a man's game. 'Comments disagreeing with my views saying, "typical woman, knows nothing about football".'

'Another female fan once accused me of only being interested in football to "shag men".'

'The most common example is when you are talking football with a group of men and there is always one who asks if you know the offside rule. It happened once when I was with my uncle and he turned round to the guy and said "my niece is a qualified football coach are you?" He shut up straight away!'

'Aimed at a female assistant referee, a man sat in front of me shouted for her to get back to the kitchen. Despite her making a correct decision.'

'People are always shocked that I like football and try to catch me out by asking me questions like "what's the offside rule?" Or "who is such and such?" They aren't major things but they are so sexist and it really, really grates on me.'

'People amazed that I have a season ticket for over 20 years … because I'm a girl. Also, people amazed I can talk football all day and know the rules.'

'Males assuming that I'm not a proper fan or interrogating me to "prove" my support.'

'Rude comments/sexist comments due to being a female attending games.'

'Being told you belong in the kitchen and the chants of "get your tits out for the lads"; it's disgusting.'

'It's the usual "explain the offside rule if you know about football". I play too, in National League in goal, and I've lost count of the amount of "get back in kitchens" I've heard, "women's footballers can't beat 14-year-old boys … "women can't play on this pitch cause it's for the boys" …'

'A coach-full shouting "get your tits out".'

'I've been going to football since 1975 so there is a lot to list. When I was younger it was, I must be going to football because I fancied the players or I was after a boyfriend. Later it was I must be gay and that's why I liked football. Even later when I was married it was "your husband must be dragging you along to games – wouldn't you rather be shopping?" "Can you explain the offside rule" is also another favourite? Whatever the approach, whenever I said I love football, there would often be a challenge – like "can you name the left-back who played one game in 1948", ridiculous stuff that very few people would know. It was always about trying to make me feel uncomfortable. But I'm still here.

'On Twitter I'm always told to stay in the kitchen along with my opinions. If ever I tweet about football it's like, "well what's the offside rule?"'

'In person I regularly go to games on my own, I'm always

looked at differently. Called "darling", "sweetheart" like "are you lost darling?" "No hun I'm here just the same as you." Even comments like "oh I didn't think you'd know this much" annoy me cause I'm like "well why?" My gender shouldn't play a part.'

'Males/men from other fan-bases verbally abuse women/girls who love and follow football. We're constantly told to get back in the kitchen and also told to do the household chores just because we love and support our club and football in general. Just cause I have a vagina I get abused for my love of the sport and [told] I should go support another type of sport other than football.'

'Young lads at an away game (who were drunk) disagreeing with everything we said at the game saying we didn't know what we were talking about.'

'Remarks about women not knowing what they're talking about when it comes to football, remarks about women staying in the kitchen, remarks about football not being for women, remarks about makeup, remarks about women's bodies, remarks about how women should have "sexier kits to make men interested in them playing", etc etc.'

'"Get your tits out" chants from men at football. Standard kitchen comments and dismissal of opinion. I could probably come up with an essay!'

'Being shouted at during games (asked to flash, asked if I sleep with players, asked which players I am attracted to, asked to wear tighter clothes and comments made about my figure or general appearance). Lots of lewd comments. I have also been touched inappropriately or had overtly sexual behaviours directed at me included being flashed by crowd members. I generally always have my role in football connected to whether I have a partner/how my boyfriend feels about me being involved in male football. I have been sent inappropriate messages on social media (pictures of male genitalia) which is probably my worst experience; when the behaviour was directly flagged as being inappropriate, I was made to feel that I was being "over sensitive". It's not easy being a female physio in the male football game!'

'The usual "get your tits out" stuff mostly.'

'Being told I know nothing about football because I'm a girl … or apparently know a lot considering I'm a girl.'

'I've had sexual gestures made at myself when out in pubs pre match.'

'Just being told I can't wear football shirts because they're an item of clothing for men, being told my opinion doesn't count as I don't really understand the sport, I should be going to women's games not men's games. I shouldn't be shouting at games cos it's unladylike I should be at home making my partner a meal for when he gets in.'

'Female referee assistant being shouted at, by a fan near me standing on the terraces. He said "that's why women have no place in football."'

'When commenting on a football post on Facebook I was told to "get back in the kitchen". Before, I've been told that I only like football to impress men or that I must be a lesbian if I like football. When stating that I like football, men ask me ridiculous questions like "well if you support xyz, who is your manager?"'

'Online belittling of knowledge or real interest in the sport due to gender.'

'I see the online abuse that female football presenters and pundits get! Being told that they only have the job because they are a woman!'

'I've also felt very uncomfortable while outside the ground [with people] sniggering, whispering in front of me. Blokes choosing to disengage in a debate or conversation about football with me. Where they will speak to others.'

'Whilst stood on the terraces I've had men shout at me that women don't swear or come to football. I've had "get in the kitchen" type messages on social media.'

'When attending an away game, I received sexist abuse from opposition fans as I walked down the road (alone, midday kick-off) towards the stadium.'

'I have been at football grounds (L2 and National League) where there are no female stewards available for fan searches. Fans often told no search no entry and can feel pressured into allowing a member of the opposite sex to search them. I have not done this, but I have been told I will not enter the ground as I refused a search.'

'Been given funny looks when celebrating a goal because I'm a girl.'

'Got called a "mong"' and got told to get back to the kitchen for having an opinion on something which a male didn't agree with.'

'I have had men tell me "You don't know what you're talking about, you're only a woman" or a common one was "name a football player other than Ronaldo".'

'Also been sexualised for liking football, by saying I'm more attractive for liking football. Or whether I can send picture in just a football shirt.'

'Pretty much any time I disagree with a male over a footballing opinion, they make a sexist remark. "Get back in the kitchen" "go make me a sandwich" "go wash the pots" etc.'

'It has actually affected me to the point I no longer interact as much as I would like to on social media around football. I used to be very comfortable sharing my opinions but know I will always receive a "what do you know you're a girl" type response so have stopped sharing my views as I can't be bothered to deal with the negative sexist responses back. The maddening thing is I played for a women's team up until Covid put a halt to our season and would still be told I don't know anything about football. "Do you even know the offside rule?" … "erm, yes I have to make sure I'm not offside every Sunday when I play …"

'I've been asked to "get my tits out for the lads". Also wolf whistling …'

'When I used to write the programme I used to get all the time that I didn't know what I was talking about because I was female. I hear it all the time aimed at younger, prettier females than me. Being a bit older now I don't get it and neither does my mum but when we were younger we used to get it all the time.'

'Female line assistants and referees get chanted at "get yer tits out for the lads".'

'Online, I have a few times replied to men making comments about eg women footballers getting back to the kitchen. I have tried to explain how sexist stereotype jokes like this actually hold women back as it feels like one step forward, two steps back. Every single time I've tried to respond calmly explaining, I've been met with "it's only a joke, love".'

'I always see comments such as "what do you know you're a woman" not aimed at me but I've seen it happen online.'

'I have seen casual sexist behaviours directed towards my female coaches I worked with, dismissive of their ability because of their gender. I've also seen them spoken down to for the same reason when they share their opinion in the pub or at the game.'

'In my younger days being asked to "get my tits out for the lads". Being told I don't have a valid point because I am a woman.'

'I posted my opinion of a game on social media and a male fan had a go at me saying I didn't know what I was on about despite the fact I was at the game! When I've been at matches my family and work colleagues have my back but it doesn't stop male fans making comments about how I know nothing about football and being offended that I sometimes know more than they do.'

'I've answered "no" to whether I've received sexist abuse online, however, I don't voice my opinion online often. When I've spoken about football at the gym before if there was a conversation about it, I've been ignored or chuckled at by a man, who then proceeded to talk to my boyfriend about the exact topic I just spoke about.'

'Had to go on my own to one match where it was worse than other times. Comments during match made me feel uncomfortable.'

'Being treated like a silly woman who has no real interest in the game or opinions worth listening to. Also lack of facilities such as ladies' loos.'

'Online tweets, inappropriate gestures, generic speaking down, made to feel like I have to "prove" myself.

'I've seen comments online aimed at other female fans/players/ media and heard general chants and comments (not directed at myself) while watching games.'

'I've witnessed female officials being called names and supporters asking her "where's your ironing board" or "show me where you piss from."'

'I have seen a male Wolves fan sharing tweets about women's football and basically claiming they are clueless based on their gender, this resulted in me blocking him as it really frustrated me seeing a comment like that online.'

'I have had different things said to me at the pub and in the towns of away games. I have been belittled for following football and made to feel like I don't belong at times. I have heard things such as "you don't know anything about football as you're a girl", "get back in the kitchen" and "get your tits out for the lads."'

'There's been a few experiences, the worst ones were from away fans, Chesterfield at home someone held a flag up calling me a slag, I was included in a group chat with Carlisle fans and my dad's death mocked, I've been told that I know nothing and hated because I'm a girl who loves football, I've been told I shouldn't be there as I'm a girl, I was told it's for attention etc years later I'm still there!'

'If women go to football they should be seen, not heard.'

'I was once hurt (accidentally) at football and the guy who did it didn't apologise – I confronted him and his words were "you shouldn't be here anyway".'

'I was refused to join in a social conversation once because "you wouldn't know anything about football".'

'If you're a woman and you want to watch football, why don't you just watch women's football.'

'Told that I only go to games for male attention and had drunk men think it's okay to say/do what they want in concourses and been told online to get back in the kitchen and my opinion is invalid because I'm a girl.

'I am always being told to "get back in the kitchen" and referred to as a "bird" when discussing football. My boyfriend gets a lot of stick too due to me voicing my opinion as he "should keep me quiet".'

'When I first joined a football forum aged 18 so many inappropriate comments were made. There was even a "fittest Gas babe" poll set up to rate the female fans. Lots of little comments throughout my time watching football and men assuming I'm only watching football because my boyfriend dragged me there.'

'At the stadium, I was called "fucking bitch, you should be at home making tea".'

'Every single day without fail, I see sexist abuse towards women online. Whether it's myself or someone else. The abuse ranges from "get in the kitchen" all the way to death threats.'

'Seen it in the media, sexist abuse to the female commentators. In football grounds over the years, been leered at, had sexist comments made. The assumptions that because I am a woman I don't understand football, or the offside rule. Also been to lots of grounds over the years where the toilets for women have been just disgusting.'

'1) Whilst watching football with my partner (a non-football fan) a man stood in front of me and said to my partner, "it's okay, she doesn't care about football anyway". He was corrected and then told me I should be in the kitchen whilst laughing in my face! 2) Have heard chanting about female officials, about them being below par. 3) Several men told me that if I wanted to be a fan I should "get my t*ts out for them". 4) Told by a fellow fan that I only go to the football to watch footballers not the game, he then proceeded to wink and laugh. 5) Had a man grab my boobs during a goal celebration. 6) Had a man rub his groin on my backside. Sadly the list goes on!'

'Been told to get back in the kitchen (classic), "oh good for you, must get all the boys because you like football",' been called a boy/lesbian, cat-called, been told I don't know the offside rule, the list goes on!'

'Have heard it from opposition supporters but not directly to me. Would like to see an end to "get your tits out for the lads".'

'Comments such as "what do you know about football, you're a girl", "it's a male thing", "stick to what women do best".'

'I've been questioned and quizzed as to whether or not I know the offside rule, the starting line-up of my team, the club's history etc.'

'When I express my opinion on players, that men don't agree with, I get told that my opinion is redundant and I am a stupid girl.'

'People say that I attend my club's football matches for "social media clout" and not for the fact that it's my passion.'

'"I bet you don't even know the offside rule" is a common one. I've been called a slut/slag/whore for no apparent reason at away games. Also, men who make you "prove" your knowledge by asking you bizarre trivia. My own fan base is actually very supportive, this normally comes from away fans/random men in the pub. And just general disbelief that a girl in her 20s has an interest in, is knowledgeable on and enjoys football.'

'I was once told I was "entertainment" for the team on the way home, because I'm female. It links to this assumption that we only go to football to impress boys etc.'

'It was one of my first away games and I was young, maybe 12/13. There was a guy behind my dad and me, hurling abuse at the team, but then it turned to my father and me. Most of the abuse was towards my father, but I also remember him [the man] constantly saying "she shouldn't be here, she doesn't know what she's on about. She's a girl she should be shopping" etc., which hurt my dad! After it turned on me, luckily my dad stood up for me! How is a 12-year-old meant to deal with sexist verbal abuse! This definitely put me off going to away games for a while. But I'm very lucky that that has been my only abuse … touch wood.'

'Myself and two other girls went to Portugal for the Nations League a few years ago and had a few snide comments from so-called England fans. "Oh didn't realise girls were on this train too, what are you doing here?" Also posted a photo of us and our England and Rovers flag on Twitter and had sexist comments.'

'Starting a chant at the football and someone on Facebook asking "who gave the woman the song sheet?". Repeated sexual comments about me. Being told to go back to the kitchen. Being mistaken as the tea lady at a game where I was a guest in the boardroom.'

'I haven't experienced it myself but I have seen many comments online, especially with females who support football, [people] saying they only support the team because they fancy a player or are trying to impress men. Growing up I have tried to get involved in football conversations with men I know and I always feel as though they never value my option due to being a female, most of the time I actually know more than most men but they just don't take my opinions on board. Also when people haven't liked my opinion on Twitter, the comments back are always "slag" or "stupid bitch", which is only because I'm a female. If I tell people I like football they always say "oh is it because of your husband or your dad", when I actually support a completely different team to them.'

'I was at a game and asked the guy behind me to stop leaning over my shoulder trying to shout at the goalkeeper. He was literally screeching in my ear! He turned on me and was screaming in my face saying that I was a "stupid slag". Things escalated and stewards removed the man.'

'As a teenager (so many years ago) being groped standing on the terraces, getting felt up on a crowded tube on the way to the ground. Having "get your tits out for the lads" directed at me and my (female) school friends. Nowadays, well into middle age and often at games with my husband, although I do sometimes go alone, I am covered by a cloak of invisibility!'

'When I was at an England game, this Pompey fan said to me I shouldn't be allowed to go to games due to being a woman and also told me to sit down as I wouldn't know the rules, bearing in mind I was only 18 years old.'

'I commented on some posts about my team on Facebook and a guy told me I didn't know anything because I am a woman.'

'I also coach football sessions and have seen little girls say "the boys say girls can't play football".'

'In the school team I fought hard to play in the boys' team and was told several times I shouldn't play as I'm a girl.'

'It is generally pretty low-level abuse but has been pervasive my entire life. Similar comments to those you highlighted on the video, like querying whether I know the offside rule, if I'm only into football to get male attention, asking me to name the squad or give details of past trophies to test my knowledge etc etc. However there have been some more serious incidents. Markedly at a live game at Elland Road, when I was in the away end when I was about 20, me and two female friends were pinned into a corner and pushed physically by a number of male Leeds fans, with abusive and sexual language being used as well as physical intimidation. We had to be "rescued" by some male friends but it did put me off from attending away games just with female friends for a good while. And I've never been to Elland Road again!'

'Been called slag and fat, all because I had a difference of opinion to a couple of men.'

'I've been a referee during a game years ago and was met with sexist abuse from the players because I didn't give a foul.'

'I used to coach U7s and children's parents would ask if I was a woman over text before coming to training; all was well until they knew I wasn't a man. Some would turn up and never show again. The parents of the kids I was coaching would overpower [them] and the kids would listen to them.'

'A male referee got my allocated referee games, despite not being appointed for the match (he just happened to be there, in kit).'

'These are just a few of my experiences … I've been told to keep away from the men's game, it's not made for me; I only know what I know because it's what the men are saying; I've been told my opinions are wrong because I'm a woman. "No penis no opinion" is something I've been told [and that] I only follow football to try and gain male followers/popularity.

'Regular comments made online – "you only go to football for the lads, you're attention-seeking, do you even know the offside rule?". When at away games, we would have lads staring at us, wolf whistling etc. When walking to my seat I have been brushed on the bum before. Away fans shouting abuse at us.

'I had a lot of men be derogative towards me and my friend, that females are allowed in pubs for match days, saying to a partner who supports the same team that I should be in the kitchen and not at football. Asking what the offside rule is, just not being allowed an opinion really.

'Shocked that a woman like me is into football when we have been all over Europe and also in terms of that women go to football for male attention.

'I have experienced comments such as "get your tits out", or "alright love" suggestively, wolf whistles.'

'I also think there is at times a real lack of respect for women with things such as watching England away, when the women's toilets are quieter, men thinking it acceptable to use them instead and doing so whilst on show with the doors open.'

'I've been told to go back to the kitchen, called for my looks and weight. And even threatened with physical assault.'

'Comments at pubs are probably more common than from our own fans in the ground – but usually involve comments suggesting women don't know what football is or that they should be at home. Often been asked if my boyfriend knows I'm out as well!'

'Accused on many occasions that I don't enjoy football and that I pretend, to get male attention. Critiqued over my opinions as a female, way more than my male counterparts. Told I don't know what I'm talking about, as I'm a female. Been told to "get back into the kitchen".'

'I have always been challenged on whether I know as much as men, such as "what's the offside rule then" etc. I am not massively feminine, which I think saves me from the abuse in stadiums being so overt. Often remarks saying "get back to the kitchen", "you wouldn't know, it's a men's game" or that I only go to games for "male attention". On Twitter if someone doesn't agree they sometimes add "plus you're a woman".

'In the past I've received lots of comments in terms of how do I know so much because I'm a girl, why am I in the pub watching football by myself, why do I invest so much time into it because I'm a girl and I should be doing other things. As you can imagine I've received a lot of shit just for my chosen clubs in general, let alone being a girl!'

'Just the typical comments, "you belong in the kitchen", "you're only pretending to like football to get guys' attention", "women shouldn't like football".'

'Too many to share even half of them.'

'Opposition fan pushed me against a wall and said I was asking to be raped when I disagreed with his opinion about the game.'

'Heard a fan on the terrace shout "the only thing you're good for is your tits" at Sian Massey-Ellis when she ran the line at one of our FA Cup games.'

'Told to "get back in the kitchen" or "get your tits out" more times than I can keep count of.'

'Told husband and I are "the wrong way round" and "don't know why he puts up with it" because on Saturdays he likes to go shopping while I go to football, and because he looks after our children while I go to away matches (I take them to home ones).'

'My club used to host "gentlemen's evenings" where sports personalities would come to speak and women weren't allowed to attend. They sometimes did "ladies' nights" too, which were just cabaret, nothing to do with football.'

'Asked opposition players their opinions on some of our tactics, they just stared at me then one of them said "fancy a spit-roast love?"'

'When I buy the same football-ground food as the male fans (pies, chips, burgers) people always comment things like "aren't you watching your figure?" "Dear me that doesn't look very healthy", "eating AGAIN?", "are you going to eat ALL of that? Pig," which nobody ever says to the men. I stopped eating at matches because of this, I prefer to go hungry.'

'Why do you really go to football? You must like looking at the players' legs in their shorts.'

'I was interviewed on a national sport radio station about a fundraiser I was doing for my club which involved cycling to all the away matches. When he found out going to all the home and away matches was something I did every season the presenter said "so you like football then!" in a surprised tone, then asked if I had a boyfriend and whether he minded me doing this.'

'Being heckled in pubs or at the ground.'

'Been told on social media I don't have a clue what I'm talking about on countless occasions, "get back to the kitchen and make a sandwich", been told in person at a game before "shut the fuck up you don't know what you're on about", been told "you only watch football for male attention".'

'When I was walking to the ground a little boy said "why is that girl going to football?"'

'Comments of a sexual nature on club coaches, inappropriate chanting of a sexual nature by supporters of my team, comments about my football knowledge being lesser than males.'

'I remember being in a pub once with my partner and a few friends. It was the Merseyside derby. I support Everton and my partner supports Liverpool. I remember pointing out that one of the Liverpool players was offside and this man (who was not with us) laughed in my face and said "shut up love, you don't even know what offside is. Get back in the kitchen". A lot of men nearby found it funny. My partner was at the bar at the time so was not privy to the comments. I was quite shocked by this and it upset me.'

'Well, I'm a coach of a football team and the team and I are one huge family … so there's no problem at all. Even though I'm the youngest and I'm a woman, I can handle them pretty well. But sometimes, especially when I started being a coach, a few old grandpas (age 65+) or older fans (age 50+), started to say "oh she slept with them, so she can be a coach" or "yeah, he might get some extra lessons after the game." I mean … on the one hand I can understand why people say that, cause I'm 20, a woman and a coach of a team which is age 19-32, but if you know the background stories you know EXACTLY why I am here: that is what keeps me motivated. On the other hand, I really don't understand why people don't shut the f**k up, when they know nothing. At the end, I'm glad I can now say that is no longer a problem, because everybody knows me and everyone can see what impact I have on my team and I'm so proud to call them my family.'

'Always "what do you know about football you're a girl" and "fuck off back to the kitchen".'

'You don't know anything about football because you're a girl.'

'You only follow football for the men.'

'I regularly see male Twitter users commenting sexist things on videos of women playing football and I overhear a lot of negativity towards the women's game. I can't think of specific examples of things that have been said or tweeted but the gist of it is that they pinpoint a bad performance from a female football game, go out of their way to put together clips of poor shots or poor gameplay and imply that this is what makes up the entirety of women's football. These compilations or videos are then followed by an entourage of "crying with laughter" emojis and quotes like "this is why we don't take women's football seriously" or "they're a joke". I've never seen these same types of people put together videos of male players and attack them in the same way as the female players. You often hear men talking about how all women who play football must be lesbians or that they don't look "lesbian enough to play football".'

'You should have been born a boy.'

'I've been told to get back in the kitchen, get back to laundry and get back to looking after my kids (I don't have any!). I get told regularly that my opinion isn't relevant as females don't understand football. I've been called a bitch, a slag and a stupid whore just for daring to state my views. It's tiring and hurtful.'

'Just the usual barrage of sexist "banter" about not knowing the rules of the game, comments about the size of my breasts in a football shirt, assuming it's my husband who's the football fan.'

'To generalise, some men have a problem with a woman having football knowledge and make it clear they aren't welcome in online discussions or meets.'

'Once on a supporters' coach travelling to a game (not one I've been with since) me and my friends were told that we shouldn't be going to football because we were women; they even started a chant about "kicking women out of football". This was quite a few years ago but has really stuck. Told to take our tops off/bras off as a "funny" chant.'

'When coaching an under-8s team a few years ago had comments from an opposition team about being a female coach and online from the same team about being laughed at for us having two female coaches. Also had comments from referees at junior games about "looking good when wet" when raining and comments like "I wish we had coaches like you when I was younger". Just made to feel really uncomfortable even by doing volunteer work. I don't coach anymore to avoid these things. I was around 17 at the time too.'

'At football matches (especially away matches) being touched on the concourse and in the queues by people behind in the queue.'

'Being told I don't know anything about football because I'm female and my opinion isn't valid.

I have had people questioning whether I like football or just think it's "cool". Had jokes made about me not knowing the offside rule.'

'I've had the usual comments – "get back in the kitchen", "stick to make up", "you know nothing". I've been accused of doing "favours" for tickets when the reality is that I built up my own credits on my membership card and made some amazing friends along the way so I am able to follow Liverpool home and away. Working in football for a while also helped. I was sexually assaulted on a European trip by people I thought were friends and would take care of me and it has been shrugged off by everyone who was there and knew about it.'

'Remarks from men as passing at games and laughing as if I don't know what I am doing, also whistled at while walking to the ground. Also being added to Twitter group chats where they rate you etc.'

'I got asked what I was doing here and shouldn't I be at home doing the dishes. I've also been sexually objectified in a public place because of my love for football.'

'I have been told I can't have an opinion because I'm a woman, I need to get back in the kitchen and I will never make it in the industry.'

'Sexist chants towards female officials.'

'Groped at games.'

'Walking through the stand and a group of boys shouted "Get your rat out" (I'm assuming that's referring to my lady parts lol).'

'Tweets mainly saying "get back to the kitchen", football fans ranking women and girls on Twitter in terms of whether they would have sex with them, questioning knowledge because of my gender.'

'Received serious backlash after using a gender-neutral phrase instead of "linesman", was told I was sensitive/woke/snowflake for wanting to be inclusive of female officials.'

'At a pub in London before Tottenham away a few years ago, my mum and I both had comments made on how we looked and that we were only there "for a day out" and we "can't be there to just watch the football". Comments online have been worse, get called a slag for making a joke about another team or just get told "get back to the kitchen".

'I'm 34, so I've had many years of "do you even know the offside rule" or "watch the women's team" or "you only pretend to like football". I remember one time in particular at the pub, I was in my Arsenal shirt getting looks for jumping up and shouting, and Theo Walcott had done this sensational run down the pitch and I said "that was a Thierry Henry run", [then] moments after[wards] the commentator said the same thing. Suddenly everyone was cheering and wanting to buy me a drink saying "you know your stuff" and whilst that was great, I couldn't help but think when a men made comments like that, it wasn't celebrated like some amazing thing. Was it because I'm a woman? That moment always sticks in my mind with a bittersweet taste.'

'Also had the generic asking about knowing the offside rule, and whether I actually go to games (I've been a STH for four years and went with my dad periodically whilst at school too).'

'I'd get DMs on Twitter questioning my knowledge on football because "I'm a girl", comments like "you know your stuff for a girl", I'd even get DMs asking if I could explain the offside rule, on top of this, I have been called names about my appearance and generally been insulted.'

'I used to be very active on Twitter in the years 2014-18, I'd tweet multiple times a day about my team, now because of what I experienced back then I only usually tweet when my team plays, just because it only takes one person to disagree and belittle you, and it can make you feel horrible!'

'Too many to count. In person, sexist chants when walking to the ground. Online is worst though. I've had death and rape threats purely for sharing my opinions on football – ranging from anonymous football Twitter accounts from young lads to older men with their names in their profiles. I've been told all the usual stuff – "you only watch football for male attention", "you don't know the offside rule", "get back in the kitchen".'

'Equally I get sexualised for being into the sport and playing games like football manager, which is irritating.'

'Questions/remarks I have encountered – why am I not at home doing the washing. What does a woman know about football, how can you be an agent when you are a woman, are you into football because you want a boyfriend, what's your Only Fans, can I fuck you, I didn't know you women were allowed to be agents, I will let you speak to my players if you meet me. I could go on but that's some examples of what I've experienced.'

'Being questioned on the offside rule and players in my team. Told to go and get the drinks in and make them a sandwich. I could list endless comments that I have faced, that we have all faced.'

'Had a really nasty experience with some Colchester United fans in a pub in London, who got really personal about females going to football.'

'Often on Twitter if you post anything to do with sport you get responses saying that "you don't know what you're talking about".'

'I find away games more toxic than home games for abuse. Fans seems to target you as a woman as not knowing what is going on/understanding the game etc.'

'I personally find a lot in the industry I work in being predominantly male based, football "banter" is often meant to go over my head, and I get comments from males when I try to join in as if to say, "do you even understand what we're joking about".'

'I haven't had any sexist comments towards me but I see a lot of comments online saying women only belong in the kitchen, Villa women have had death threats and men just tasking the p*** out of everything a woman does on the pitch etc.'

'I have been asked "oh does your boyfriend support Norwich?" even though I don't have one and was evidently there of my own accord; I've also had "No wonder you support Norwich if you're a female football fan, not a proper team". I frequently get the comment "oh you're a girl and you know about football" after people try to grill me about football trivia. I have had a lot of comments online about my voice if I post a video of me chanting along, comments that a guy definitely wouldn't get.

I do want to say most of the abuse is from non-Norwich fans. I have never had an incident at Carrow Road.'

'Just "aha you're girl you probably know nothing about it".'

'I used to have Twitter but decided to delete it because I'd get sexist comments after I posted something about football so it was easier to just remove myself from Twitter altogether.'

'I've been told I'm not allowed to have an opinion because I'm a woman. That my opinions are wrong because of my gender. I vividly remember being called "a stupid thick woman" after tweeting my opinions after a game.'

'Sexist abuse online on Twitter and on YouTube. I've been made to feel uncomfortable watching football in the pub too.'

'I was told a woman supporting and following football makes as much sense as a chocolate teapot.'

'People have attacked my body image on social media because Bristol Rovers lost.'

'I have had comments in secondary school from boys and teachers asking me why I support football and that I should be doing something else on a weekend.'

We then asked the women if there was anything they'd like to add or whether there's anything specific they'd like to see from #HerGameToo moving forward!

Here's what some of them had to say:

'Firstly, I think this campaign is so fantastic and love the unity and togetherness you have created. I would love to connect with more people who support different teams if that could somehow be made possible through the platform.'

'I've supported my club since I was 11, I've been a season ticket holder for many of those years and I feel in the last few years sexism has gotten worse, always online stuff from keyboard warriors. I've always felt comfortable going to games and never experienced anything unpleasant either home or away.'

'More women officials.'

'Emphasise that it is nearly always the faceless social media accounts that give the sexist abuse, as I have a season ticket and have never experienced it in person at Old Trafford.'

'I've been attending football matches for nearly 50 years and would like some progress to be made to encourage young women to play, watch and comment on football without prejudice. Things haven't changed much in those 50 years.'

'Possibly more on the experiences of queer women, disabled women or women of colour in football? No criticism of the campaign at all because I think it's great, just a suggestion.'

'I think this movement is amazing and it is so important that sexism in football is being spoken about!! I would love to see merch created for this campaign!!'

'I would love for my daughter to be able to grow up enjoying all sports and feeling like an equal.'

'I'd like to see more players engage with the campaign. I was really disappointed when none of the players I admire posted anything about the women's world cup when it was on. Their endorsement would have been so influential.'

'We need to see more female representation on mainstream media and in important job roles within the industry! Merch would be great … maybe team-specific merch too? Great for match days … supporting your team and the #hergametoo movement!'

'It's fantastic to see the campaign. We are very lucky because our local club has both boys' and girls' football at junior level but there is still an obvious divide between the sexes. All clubs need to treat both sexes equally.'

'Football needs to change, and we need men to be allies. Why is it inherently such a bad thing to be a woman in football or a female fan? I know it exists, but we need to hold all fans accountable and make sure that sexist abuse gets reported, and also that it is dealt with, especially by regulators and clubs themselves.'

'I like that the video you made put faces to the people who receive sexist abuse; I think when people type it online they forget there is a real person on the receiving end.'

'I have seen a reduction in sexist abuse at grounds (for example I don't think I would hear "Get your tits out for the lads" sung from a terrace to a young woman in the away end these days) and I am of an age where I am confident to challenge young men in my home end, if they start a chant about, for example, the opposition manager's wife. I think fans should be encouraged to self-police but they can only do this with confidence if stewards will back them up. I therefore think fans and stewards need more education on respect for women (and others subject to abuse). The latent misogyny is much more blatant online and it is not just football related. I would like to see young boys and girls educated about respect for women (and others subject to abuse) throughout primary and secondary education. The joy of football is that it is all about opinions and women should be able to engage in debate online. I loved your video and would love to see more. Perhaps somehow demonstrating how reactions differ to comments made by men and women? Perhaps by showing the different responses to the same comment if voiced by a woman and then by a man?

'I think including older female fans, possibly historical footage of women enjoying the football, helps strengthen the point that our game is for everyone and always has been.

'Maybe highlight the diversity in women's football including people from different backgrounds.

More of what you're doing anyway! Amplifying the voices of female fans, women playing football at all levels – from all over and of all ages. Reiterating that we belong here, and we're staying. Football is for everyone, there's room for all of us, but not for abuse, as well!'

'Make women more comfortable within the football industry/ social media.'

'Pressure on governing bodies and clubs to crack down on sexist comments.'

'There is an amazing amount of work going into women watching and supporting but it feels very centred in the men's game, maybe we could have more about what's going on in the women's game and promoting what they're doing.'

'I enjoy the blog posts on the website. You should reach out to every single club and ask them to get involved, I'd love to see my team (Peterborough) involved! They have a ladies' team and I think they would retweet content.'

'The lack of female-targeted football kit available/on sale in shops, sportswear outlets.'

'To keep up the excellent work and visibility of the issue.'

'I'd like to see Her Game Too really focus on not just the female supporters but the women's game as there is a lot of discrimination towards the women's game!'

'Wider spread coverage on the fact this is still an on-going problem for female players. People are so naive that we've progressed massively because of brand campaigns when reality is that there is a long way to go, in terms of education and equal rights.'

'It's a great initiative. Keep going! We have the right to talk about football too. We owe it to the next generation of girls all around the world.'

'Be more visible at grounds.'

'Keep up the hard work. Educate people, as to what is sexist. The difference between banter with people you know is very different from the typed word to a stranger.'

'The Chelsea men's team ran out to the Chelsea women's team on their podium recently and celebrated their championship win with them. This I saw on TV and thought that's so important for these knuckle draggers to also see their men's team behaving in this manner. Supporters' forums must have a quota of women on them, like the way the TV channels are attempting to redress the balance across gender for presenters. Any bad words or inflammatory language from these horrible and abusive men needs to be red-carded by social media, in the pubs, in the grounds. Needs to be put into law it's an offence to speak and treat women like this.'

'The #HerGameToo campaign is a big step forward for us female football fans, as well as female footballers. Women in the football industry have been abused for their football opinions for far too long now and it's great to see a campaign taking a stand!'

'More personal stories from women around the world!'

'Just more of it, it's brilliant and highlighting that women are still getting treated differently in 2021! My daughter is 11 and plays in a school team, she's the only girl, they got to the semi-final and the opposing team said "omg they have a girl in defence, we are going to win this" her teacher said "well little do they know, she's our best player". They won the game. This was boys of 10/11 years old – enough is enough.'

'Let's make it socially acceptable for women to be involved in football just as much men are. We know what we are talking about.'

'Mix of age ranges and ethnicity shown. Link up with community programmes in clubs (Everton have an excellent one Everton in the Community) to get more leverage.'

'Tackle the presumptions that many people make because you're a woman who likes football. i.e. you must be a lesbian, you're just pretending and trying to impress a guy etc.'

'Link with women's football teams and fans' forums. Continuing to bring to life the examples and experiences faced as I feel it's sometimes so embedded in culture, men don't realise what they are saying is problematic.'

'Just more understanding from men about women in football.'

'To try and instill within people that just because you're a woman, it doesn't make you any less knowledgeable or talented about football. Plenty of men are absolutely clueless but because they're men no one bats an eyelid. However, if we came out with something similar we would be condemned for it.'

'Just for more opportunities for girls and women to get into playing or even coaching the sport they love.'

'Carry on raising awareness – some people don't realise how often sexist abuse goes on.

I think it would be really great if there could be factions of the campaign up and down the country for each team, or even just areas, South Yorkshire, north east, etc ... Group chats, pre-match meet-ups. All very inclusive to women from every background. It would definitely take some work but would make a massive difference to the community, safety in numbers and all that. Also be pleased to see the campaign raise issues from female fans from minorities. Disabled women, women of colour, etc.'

'Would love to see some voices and opinions from older women eg 40/50+ and see what their experiences are like today and whether the abuse is more targeted at younger people. I feel like I get less comments/abuse/judgement from men compared with when I was 18/19 despite following the support since I was four.'

'Keep up the good work. My daughter is nearly 13 and has played in an all-girls' team for three years. The future is bright for female football.'

'More video posts, keep up the good work!'

'I would love to see more memorabilia aimed at women. We have had the odd shirts available in women's shapes but not many. And the sizes are usually awful. Women need to be involved in the design of that.'

'Maybe encourage male supporters of the initiative Try to get celebrity involvement or involvement from grassroots clubs?'

'More acceptance of women working in football without the sexist remarks. None of it bothers me as I'm a bit older but there are a lot of younger females who may feel intimidated being put in an all-male environment and that's not fair on them.'

'Women's football clubs and women players in particular to raise awareness of abuse to females in football by campaigning to stop the abuse.'

'I'd like to see women pundits get more respect.'

'Just more people sharing the campaign to spread more awareness.'

'Just more push to have match reaction, watch-alongs, vlogs, etc that include women or only women. Not taking anything away from the men but it is all very male oriented. I think it's also important to remember that women communicate in different ways, we can see different things, our focus can be in other places on the football pitch! Doesn't mean we don't know football; it just means we see something that not all men do!'

'A celebration of all women working in sport (an event or series of posts/articles to highlight their work maybe).'

'Interviews with prominent females in the football or sport industry!!!'

'Representation of women of all shapes, sizes, ages and colour.'

'Wider acknowledgement from professionals.'

'Some older women involved. That it's not all younger women who love football, that women in their 60s, 70s and 80s love football too. My nan died at 90 she still followed Arsenal to that day. My mum is an Arsenal supporter, she is 69. Went to matches regularly until she had to move to Ireland.'

'I think what you're doing is great … maybe get some younger football fans involved too. My daughter 11 is as crazy about football as me.'

'Recognising that the vast majority of people are respectful and promoting/reinforcing this positive aspect – and growing it further – as well as addressing the issues. Encouraging all age groups to be involved too.'

'The language and foul manner of supporters at games can be aggressive and frightening. More power granted to stewards if necessary to throw people out when they are abusive in any manner.

I'd like to see more of our male counterparts joining in not by simply supporting it but by speaking out. I think for any movement to be successful and impactful the whole community (in this case the football community) stand together.'

'A push on female officiators! I lined a men's game voluntarily and got "who gave a bird the flag?", the offside rule explained and "just wave the little flag darling" despite playing football for 20 years. Also, more aimed towards youth football as I was banned from playing in the school team because the boys didn't like that they were subbed when I got to play.'

'Would love to see Her Game Too have some WOC involved in the campaign and would be great to see some events happen (in person) maybe small tournaments or something where female football fans can get involved!'

'Love the campaign, would love to see the grounds adapt their facilities to acknowledge that there are more women coming to the games now. Sexist comments should be treated in the same way as racist comments.'

'We need to get this campaign global! We need to have the views and opinions of women in sport widely available!'

'Just keep raising awareness and think about education programmes for boys/men. Most of them have sisters and mothers … why don't they make that connection that by abusing one, they abuse us all?! Since joining Twitter a couple of years ago, very late to that party, and by being very tight on whom I follow or block, it's been a really positive experience and I feel much more a part of a like-minded community.'

'A clear message: women don't want special treatment but to be treated equally.'

'Younger girls involved in order to spread the message.'

'I would like to see all clubs involved in the campaign, and encourage people to report sexist abuse as they would do for any other kind. I would also like to see clubs do more for female fans' experiences at games. For example, female toilets at grounds are always poor and generally tend to be dirty and small. I have seen some clubs provide female sanitary products such as my own (Wolves) but this is not a universal thing. I feel that things like this would provide a more equal match day experience for women.'

'Sharing stories of how girls/women got into football.'

'A lot of the sexism we experience isn't obvious overt stuff like "get back in the kitchen", it's subtle exclusion, like how people come up to me and my male friends at football and ask their opinions on the game while ignoring me. Or the "ignore him he's just a bit of a lad" culture of acceptance towards men who make women uncomfortable at football. A lot of guys are saying things like "that's only really awful sexists, ignore them" and not realising they're part of the problem. I wonder what we can do to address the more subtle side of it?'

'Maybe have a female representative from each football club (if possible).'

'More women feeling comfortable being able to voice their opinions without being oppressed by men.'

'A female supporters' group (national) and guidance how to set one up for my club and links with other clubs.'

'I'd like to see more male voices stand up for the female game and use their platforms to let people know it's not okay to shame female footballers. I'd also like people to be made aware that there is little to no money invested in female football so there's no way they can develop as fast as the men's.'

'Highlight all of the women in football and from medics to physios to nutrition experts. Highlight the size of the women's game. Show people the stats for how many women actually watch live football because I bet it's more than most people think.'

'Branching into women in women's football as opposed to just men's?'

'Talking about it more will bring the issues to light and this campaign will do exactly that. Maybe a survey for men to fill in regarding abuse they've seen or how they would react would also be helpful.'

'Women-only watch parties would be fun, and mixed events/ quizzes etc.'

'I think an educational pack to send out to schools would be so useful for little girls! I've created school packs for the Swansea City junior club so I would love to offer my help if this is an option. A blog or a forum where all female fans can connect!'

'It would be cool to get male footballers involved – purely because they can lead the way with influence. Whilst women footballers are important, I don't feel unsafe watching women's football. It's men's football I feel unsafe with. We could put together panel events via Zoom which would be good – makes people's experiences more real and more likely to be listened to.

Please include non-league fans as there are so many women out there who are involved who face abuse.'

'No idea if it's possible but I'd love pubs to get on board and have signs etc. supporting the movement and essentially implement a zero tolerance for sexist j200

bs which could help female supporters watch games without the fear of abuse.'

'Could be cool to have some pages set up for us to talk about football with each other. I love the competitive chat, sadly some men can't take it. Inspire girls into liking football, not just for men to like!'

'Love the campaign! Would be great to see more diversity so that the whole movement can be more inclusive to all women in football. Keep up the great work.'

#HerGameToo Official Survey Results Report August 2021

About Us
The #HerGameToo campaign was founded in May 2021 by Caz May and co-founded by Abbie Ackroyd, Amy Clement, Bobbi Hadgraft, Caitlin Bennett, Emily Drakeley, Eve Ralph, Hollie Harvey, Izzy Perry, Jess Furness, Leah Case and Lucy Ford.

We are committed to growing the Her Game Too campaign with the aim of fostering an ethos in football in which women are welcomed and respected equally. From fans to journalists to players to pundits, we are passionate about making football a more inclusive and safer environment for women.

The Survey
We wanted to conduct a survey to get a wider understanding of the struggles faced by female football fans in the UK. We felt it necessary before furthering the work of the campaign.

The survey was sent out to 500 women and was fully completed by 394 participants.

The survey was created and distributed via Typeform. We hoped to obtain both quantitative and qualitative data to support our campaign.

We offered total anonymity but also offered a chance for participants to leave their contact details to be sent the results and other Her Game Too updates.

www.hergametoo.co.uk

Participants

The survey was sent out to female football fans online (Facebook groups, Twitter, Instagram and via email), we received 394 responses over the few weeks the survey was live.

Age Range

Majority of participants were between 18 and 30 with the lowest representation of ages in the U18 and 60+ category.

Club

We had responses from fans all over the country.

Online Abuse

The campaign was launched off the back of overwhelming online sexist abuse. We wanted to find out more about the participants and whether they had seen or experienced any online sexist abuse.

Other Stats

We wanted to discover whether the online abuse translated to abuse in 'real life' and then how comfortable these women feel attending matches at grounds and watching in pubs. We were hoping that we would find that although abuse is experienced by women, it doesn't deter them from going to games.

We asked 'On a scale of 1–10, how comfortable do you feel watching a game at a ground. 0= wouldn't go, 10= completely comfortable':

    0 – 0%
    1 – 0.5%
    2 – 0.3%
    3 – 0.3%
    4 – 0%
    5 – 2.4%
    6 – 5.4%
    7 – 14.3%
    8 – 22.4%
    9 – 18.1%
    10 – 36.4%

We asked 'On a scale of 1–10, how comfortable do you feel watching a game at a pub. 0= wouldn't go, 10= completely comfortable':

   0 – 1.3%
   1 – 0.3%
   2 – 1.1%
   3 – 4%
   4 – 5.1%
   5 – 8.9%
   6 – 14.8%
   7 – 15.1%
   8 – 20.5%
   9 – 10%
   10 – 18.9%

We were interested (and pleased) to find that although more than half of our participants have experienced sexism whilst watching a match, the majority are still comfortable enough to go.

   We understand that the participants filling out the survey are really invested in football, regularly follow a team so may even be season ticket holders. There may be women outside of this bracket, without a vested interest in the campaign, who no longer attend or involve themselves in the football community due to the unwelcoming environment and this is something we would like to conduct more research on in the future.